M000035940

Be A Winner Trading Commodities™

Ralph J. Fessenden, Ph.D.

Personal Library

Be A Winner Trading Commodities™

Ralph J. Fessenden, Ph.D.

As with most investments, commodities trading involves risk. Despite the title "Be A Winner Trading Commodities™", persons trading commodities can lose money, including those persons who employ the strategies described in this book.

Published by
BEACON PUBLISHING, INC.
P. O. Box 770883
Naples, FL. 34107

800/207-0237
fax 941/594-1006
email: win@scaletrader.com.
website: www.BeaconWin.com

ISBN 0-9651111-1-3

Chapter 1

The Scale Trading Family

Chapter 2

Classical Scale Trading

Chapter 3

Interval Scale Trading^{SM}

Chapter 4

ParaScale Trading^{SM}

Chapter 5

Introduction to Real Market Examples

Chapter 6

August 1996 Feeder Cattle

Chapter 7

December 1996 High Grade Copper

Chapter 8

July 1998 Pork Bellies

Chapter 9

August 1998 Soybean Meal

Chapter 10

January 1998 Orange Juice

A Rollover Example

Chapter 1

The Scale Trading Family

1.1. Introduction

As a commodity trader, you are well aware of the futility of predicting when (and at what price) a top or a bottom of a market will occur. You are also well aware of the frustration of determining when a trend has started or has stopped. You can look at a chart of past price action and say to yourself "Any fool could have seen that the market was topping (or bottoming)." Yet, as the market reveals itself to you, day-by-day, it is not at all obvious what is about to happen. The more you study the price action, read the fundamentals, and ponder the advice letters, the more you realize the old adage, "If the market doesn't go up, it might go down."

Yet, you are drawn to the commodity market! The allure of the action, the enormous profits that can be made. The thrill of taking the risk. The pure and enormous satisfaction when you beat the monster in its own lair. There are few activities in this world than can give you greater pleasure than beating the market.

Trading systems abound. Some, like point-and-figure charts, date back to the late 1800's. Others, such as stochastics and neural networks, are of more recent vintage. With the advent of the computer, very sophisticated systems and plotting programs have flourished. An enormous number of these trading systems are for sale. This author receives, on the average, one advertisement a week for a trading system, which according to its blurb, will provide me with untold wealth. One can't help but wonder, "If these systems are so good, why are they being sold?"

All trading systems work, at least to a limited extent. But, to the author's knowledge, none work all of the time, nor can any produce phenomenal rewards over a period of time. In fact, most published systems don't work most of the time. The reason for this is that the markets have an ever-changing pattern that never repeats itself. Similar, yes. The same, no. Price patterns within markets are like clouds in the sky. Clouds never show the exact same shape from day to day. The shapes are similar, but always changing. You wouldn't think of trying to use today's cloud pattern to predict tomorrow's cloud pattern. Yet, in essence, that is what system traders try to do. They gather daily prices, plot them, study them, and feed them to a computer. Their goal is a prediction for tomorrow. It really isn't surprising that these folks have trouble trading commodities.

1.2. What You Must Do to Make a Profit in a Commodity Trade

Before rushing in and explaining the Scale Trading method and why it can make you money, let's back off and look at what you must do to beat the market using classical trading strategies, such as a trend following method or oscillation method. While we are at it, let's look at what you can, and cannot, predict about a commodity market.

To simplify our discussion, we are going to limit ourselves to just the long side of the market, that is, a purchase of a contract followed at a later date by its sale. To make a profit from a long position, you must:

1. Correctly anticipate that the market price is going to rise in the future;
2. Purchase a contract at a specific point in time before the price rise;
3. Hold the position (and not get faked out by a minor fluctuation);
4. Correctly anticipate that a top is about to form, or has just formed; and finally
5. Sell the contract before the price starts to decline.

Summarized, you must make three sequentially correct judgment calls:

1. That the price is about to rise
2. That the price will continue to rise, and
3. That the price is about to fall.

In addition, you must take two timely but irrevocable actions (the buy and the sell) to make a profit.

In general, the acts of buying and selling do not cause a decisive trader any problems. You can't be wishy-washy and survive in the commodity trading business. It's the three judgment calls that cause the problems. Making one or two correct calls is not good enough. You've got to be correct with all three in order to make a profit. It is a rare individual who can make all three correct judgments calls time after time.

1.3. Predicting Price Movement in a Commodity Market

Correct judgment comes from knowledge and experience. Even our gut feelings are based upon our past knowledge and experience. What do we know about the market, any market, that is true and not just something that we want to happen?

A. What We Cannot Predict

At any point in time, the market is at an equilibrium price with the instantaneous supply and demand being satisfied. It is at a price where the perceptions, hopes, and desires of the buyers are equal to those of the sellers. All known information has been digested by the traders and is reflected in the price.

In order for the market to move to a different price level, a change in perceptions, hopes, or desires of either the buyers or the sellers must occur. New information must emerge, or, the perception of old information must change. Regardless, it requires a future event to change the price.

The course of the market is truly governed by fundamental facts -- the weather, the size of the crop, pending exports, etc. This fundamental information appears in the marketplace first as rumors, then confirmed as a fact. Price change occurs during the rumor phase. It is as if the fact is leaked in small bits into the market place. Chances are excellent that you won't be privy to that information, as rumor or as fact, before almost everyone else has had a chance to act on it. Your first hint that something is going on will be a price change.

Past prices cannot be used to accurately predict future prices. What does that mean? It means that you cannot use prices to predict a top or a bottom or even the length of a trend, because the event that will cause the prices to change has not yet occurred. You cannot predict the future. No one can. Since all known information has already been reflected in a commodity's price, you can't use these prices to determine what new information might flow into the market place. This means that you can't use past prices to predict a top, a bottom, or the length of a trend. This reduces your required three judgment calls to guesses. No wonder it is so tough to make a profit in commodity trading.

B. What We Can Predict

What can we say with absolute certainty about a market? Only three things:

1. Prices will not go to zero;
2. The market will trend; and
3. The market will oscillate.

Prices will not go to zero. Commodities consist of the basic foods and related physical items that our civilization depends upon. In general, commodities are produced by a myriad of small producers, and are subject to the laws of supply and demand characteristic of all free and open markets.

Commodities are the basic food, fiber, energies and metals that our society requires for its existence. As long as our society exists, these commodities cannot have zero value. This means that between the current price and zero, there will be a price below which the price of the commodity will not drop. (See Figure 1.1.)

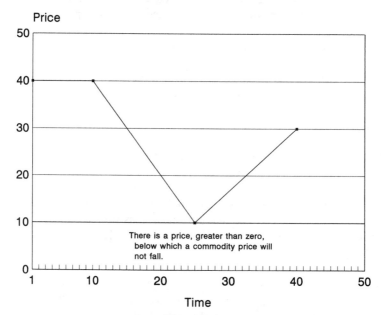

Figure 1.1
The Price of a Commodity will Not Go To Zero

Why can you expect a bottom to form? Because with commodities, there is a continuous cycle of overproduction followed by scarcity. The producers grow or produce too much, which overwhelms demand. Prices plummet. Producers get disgusted or go broke and quit producing. Demand and consumption increase because of the low prices. Scarcity develops. Prices increase. It is this fundamental cycle of which scale trading takes advantage .

The price of a commodity will not go to zero. The lower the price becomes, the greater the chance that it will bottom. You can make a rough analogy of a commodity's price to a compression spring. The more it is compressed (the price goes towards zero) the greater is its pressure for a move in the opposite direction (up).

The price at the bottom might be lower than you anticipated, but the bottom will always be there. A farmer or commodity producer can go broke, but his product, such as Wheat or Cattle, will always have some value. They never become worthless. Because of this fact, you can make an educated guess where the bottom might be for a commodity contract. The reverse statement, however, is not true. You cannot make an educated guess about a top. In times of true scarcity there is no limit to how high the price of a commodity can rise. This is why we do not scale trade from the short side of the market.

Trends. Inspection of any commodity chart will show that prices move from one price level to another over a period of time. Prices don't leap from one level to another -- rather they work their way up or down in a rather jagged fashion over a period of time. While you can predict a market will trend, you cannot predict when the trend will start, the direction the trend will take (up, down, or sideways), nor when the trend will end. Furthermore, you can't predict the magnitude of the trend. All you can truly predict is that trends will occur in the future.

Oscillations. Superimposed on the trend are oscillations, the back and forth, the little wave-like patterns observed in all freely traded markets. (Some say trends are just another, but larger, oscillation.) Like the trend, you cannot predict when an oscillation will occur, when it will end, nor its magnitude. To add to the confusion, you cannot distinguish between the start (or end) of a trend and an oscillation. As they are occurring, the two are indistinguishable. Only upon retrospect do you know which was which. However, scale trading is designed to also take advantage of these oscillations.

In summary, there are only three things you can predict about a commodity market: (1) prices will not go to zero, (2) the market will trend, and (3) the market will oscillate.

Figure 1.2 is the chart showing the daily price action of a commodity (July 1998 Orange Juice) showing an uptrend with oscillations. All free markets show the same type of price action -- trends and oscillations.

Figure 1.2
July 1998 Orange Juice- Showing an Uptrend with Oscillations

1.4. Standard Trading Methods

Considering what can be and what cannot be predicted about a market, it is not surprising that successful trading methods fall into two general groups -- trend following methods and oscillation methods.

A. Trend Following Methods

As the name implies, trend following methods attempt to identify the beginning and the end of a trend as early as possible. Because it is not possible to distinguish the beginning (or end) of a trend from an oscillation within the trend, both time and price must elapse before a position can be taken (or exited). To make a profit with a trend following method, the trend must continue for a period of time and have a fairly large price change.

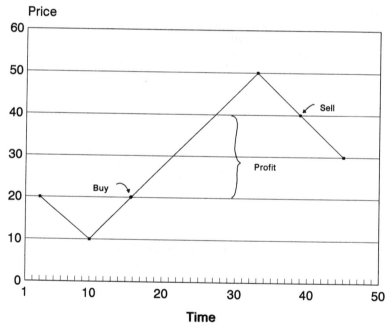

Figure 1.3
To Make a Profit with a
Trend Following Method,
The Market must have a Lengthy Trend

Profit can be enhanced if the trend following method has a sensitive method for the detection of the beginning and the end of the trend. However, the more sensitive the detection method is, the greater the number of false signals. False signals always result in a loss, which can erode profits to a great extent. To diminish the number of false signals, the trend following method can be made more conservative. This results in a smaller number of false signals, but it also results in smaller profits for the good moves. There is no satisfactory solution to this dilemma. Indeed, if the market should be very choppy, or trend in a sidewise pattern, all trend following methods will lose money.

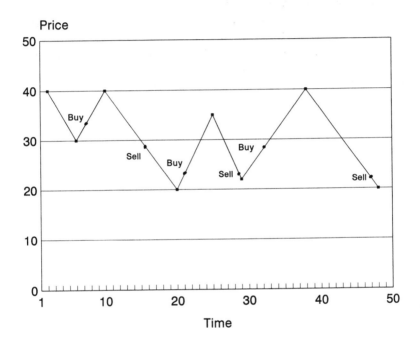

Figure 1.4
A Trend Following Method Fails when a
Market Trends Sideways or Has
Short Trends (Choppy Market)

B. Oscillation Methods

To counter the failure of the trend following methods, oscillation methods have been invented. Oscillation methods work when the market is very choppy or moving sideways. These methods signal the bottom and top of an oscillation. This allows you to buy the bottom and sell the top.

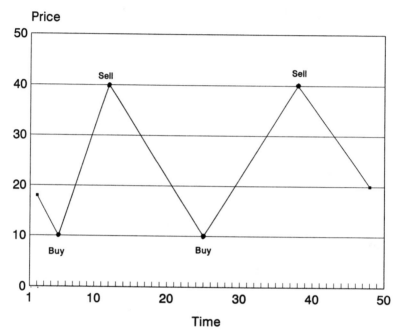

Figure 1.5
Oscillator Methods Work
Well in a Sideways Market

Oscillation methods fail when a market begins to trend. Since it is not possible to know if you are in an oscillation or the start (or end) of a trend, oscillation methods will always fail at some point in time. Relying on an oscillation method can be a very frustrating experience.

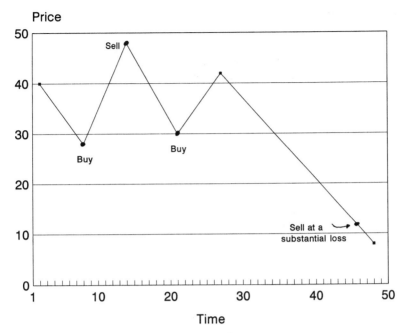

Figure 1.6
Oscillator Methods Fail in a Trending Market

1.5. The Scale Trading Family

What is so different about the Scale Trading Family of trading techniques that set them apart from other methods found in the market place? It is the assumptions that these techniques make about a market. All of the techniques in this family assume:

1. A commodity's price will not go to zero;
2. Prices move in trends, and
3. Prices will oscillate within the trend.

None of the systems in the Scale Trading Family attempt to forecast a short term high or low. All are based on the fundamental concept that once prices in a particular commodity fall low enough, market supply/demand factors will adjust so that prices will rebound once the bottom has been reached. None use stoploss orders. All require adequate capital and patience. All require an uptrend for their most profitable move. If the commodity contract does not end in an uptrend, all require a rollover into a deferred month. All have been and all will be successful in the market place. However, some are more successful than others. How do they all work?

21

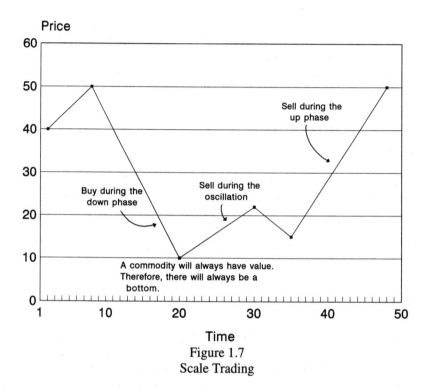

Figure 1.7
Scale Trading

With all Scale Trading techniques, we buy first then sell at a later date; that is, we only trade from the long side of a market. A long position will make money if the market goes up. However, if the market declines, we will suffer a loss.

A. Drawdown

Drawdown is the bane of Scale Traders. Drawdown is the decrease of your account's value due to a price drop of a commodity that you own. As we will see, drawdown is inherent and a natural occurrence with all Scale Trading Techniques. If you, as a scale trader, have correctly estimated drawdown, you will make a substantial amount of money. However, if you have miscalculated drawdown and underestimate the amount of capital needed, you will lose money. Indeed, if you have insufficient capital or if you lose heart and quit and have to liquidate contracts because of drawdown, you will lose a very large sum of money. In the chapters that follow, we will discuss drawdown in detail.

B. Rollovers

It is not uncommon for a commodity contract to reach its expiration date with its scale trades at a net loss. When this happens, the contracts are sold and new contracts are purchased in a more distant month. This procedure is called a *rollover*. By using a rollover, you can capture your loss along with your expected profit. Like drawdown, we will discuss rollovers in detail in the chapters that follow.

C. Members of the Family

Interval Scale Trading™ and **ParaScale Trading**™ are variations of the classical scale trading technique that reduce drawdown. With classical scale trading, there is no attempt to control drawdown. With **Interval Scale Trading**™, drawdown is controlled by using a very large interval between purchases. With **ParaScale Trading**™, drawdown is controlled by delaying the start of the trade. In this book we will cover classical scale trading first, then **Interval Scale Trading**™, and finally **ParaScale Trading**™.

Chapter 2

Classical Scale Trading

2.1. Introduction

Classical scale trading, and its variations (**Interval Scale Trading**[SM], and **ParaScale Trading**[SM]), are the three principal trading systems discussed in this book. Classical scale trading is discussed in this chapter and the variations will be discussed in subsequent chapters. In this chapter, we will use the term scale trading to refer to classical scale trading.

Scale trading was invented by Robert F. Wiest and is detailed in his book "You Can't Lose Trading Commodities" The title of the book is a little misleading, because under the proper circumstances you can indeed lose money by scale trading.

Scale trading is a mechanical trading method, requiring judgment when you begin the scale trade. With scale trading, you do not attempt to determine a short term top or bottom, nor do you attempt to determine when the prices are trending or oscillating. Scale trading is a very successful system that has shown profit in both back testing and in real time over an extended period. Unfortunately, scale trading does have a major disadvantage -- drawdown, the amount of money that is required should the commodity make a move against you. This problem is discussed in detail later in this chapter. **Interval Scale Trading**[SM] and **ParaScale Trading**[SM], the other members of the scale trading family, are designed to minimize this problem.

Let's first explain how scale trading works, then address a number of its practical features, including drawdown.

To explain scale trading we are going to use a made-up market, a pretend market rather than a real one, which will allow us to cover all the features of scale trading succinctly.

2.2. A Pretend Market to Explain Scale Trading

The price-time graph of the pretend market we are going to use for our explanations is given in Figure 2.1. It contains a downtrend, an uptrend, and an oscillation in the uptrend. We have drawn the market as if only the closes were plotted.

We have specifically excluded an oscillation in the down-trend portion of the market to simplify our explanation. This pretend market, of course, is not identical nor similar to any real market, nor is it intended to be. However, it is constructed to demonstrate the fundamental basis behind scale trading-that prices will not drop to zero and that there is some price at which supply/demand factors will adjust leading to a rebound in prices. The pretend market contains the three key features found in all real markets -- an uptrend, a downtrend, and an oscillation.

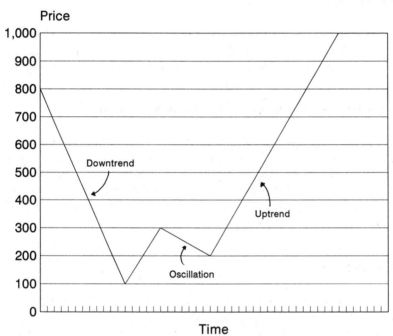

Figure 2.1
A Pretend Market to Explain Scale Trading

Keep in mind, in using this pretend market, we are armed with foresight. At any point on the time coordinate, we know what is going to happen in the "future", that is farther along (to the right) on the time coordinate. This information can color our logic and lead us to conclusions that are incorrect. The problem of knowing what is going to happen is also encountered in back-testing a trading system using historical data. In the real market, we don't know what the future holds. Therefore, in a real market at current time, we must be prepared for all contingencies. However, by using a pretend market where we can see what the "future" holds, we can explain how scale trading works and see what happens. This will allow you to understand how scale trading can be used to trade real markets where it is not known what is going to happen.

With scale trading, we only take long positions in a market. We do not take short positions. The reasons why we take only long positions and never short positions will be discussed after we have explained how scale trading works.

2.3. The Initial Steps In a Scale Trade

The steps to set up a scale trade are:

1. Select the price to begin the trading program;
2. Select the scale; and then
3. Identify the Main Buy Prices and their Levels.

A. Select the Price to Begin the Trading Program

Let's assume we select the price marked at "1, Buy" on the graph in Figure 2.3 to be our initial entry price. The technique you use to select this price in a real market will be fully discussed later in this chapter (Section 2.10). For the time being, suffice it to say that the entry point is on the lower end of a market's historical price range in order to take advantage of the expected supply/demand adjustments previously discussed and which form the fundamental basis for scale trading.

B. Select a Scale

The *scale* is the group of prices at which we are going to buy (and sell) contracts of the commodity. The specific prices at which we buy and sell are called the *Main Buy Prices*. A scale, therefore, consists of all the Main Buy Prices taken as a group. An *interval* is the difference between any two adjacent Main Buy Prices, expressed in points. In our pretend market, we will use an interval of 100 points. A *point* is a unit of price quotation. The common units of points are one dollar, one cent, and one hundredth of a cent. For our pretend market, we are going to use the value of 1 point = $10. (We will also use the term "Point" in discussing graphs. In this context "Point" means location, such as Point 1, or Point 2, to identify a specific location on a graph)

Each Main Buy Price is also identified by a Level. Levels are numbered beginning at 0. Level 0 is one interval higher in price than the Initial Buy Price, which is Level 1. Since each Level corresponds to a Main Buy Price, the number of points between any two adjacent Levels is also an interval (as defined in the above paragraph).

It is a common practice to use the term "scale" to also mean "interval". In this book, we will be consistent -- a "scale" will mean the group of Main Buy Prices and "interval" will mean the difference between two adjacent Main Buy Prices within the scale.

Figure 2.2 shows the relationship between these terms.

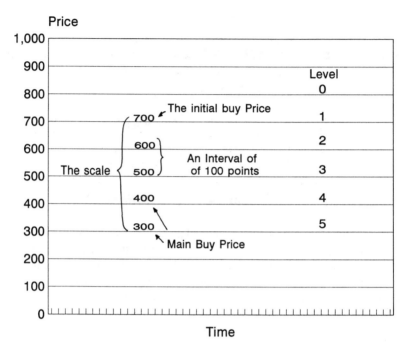

Figure 2.2
The Relationship between Scale, Main Buy Price,
Interval, and Level

C. Identify The Main Buy Points and Their Levels

These are the prices, below the current price, where we will buy an additional contract if the price drops to that level. These will also be the prices at which we will sell a contract for a profit during the uptrend. (We will explain how profits are taken shortly.) The procedure to identify the Main Buy Points and Levels are:

> 1. *The Initial Buy Price* is the price at which we begin the scale trade. This price is marked as "Buy, 1" on in the graph in Figure 2.3. (Hereafter, this location will be identified as Point 1.) This price determines Level 1, which is also marked on the graph in Figure 2.3.

> 2. *The Second Main Buy Price* is one interval below the initial entry price.

Second Main Buy Price = (Initial Buy Price) - (Interval)
                    =   500   -   100
                    =   400

The Second Main Buy Price is marked as "Buy, 2" on the graph in Figure 2.3 and hereafter will be identified as Point 2. This price determines Level 2, which is also marked as such on the graph in Figure 2.3.

3. *All Other Main Buy Prices* are determined in the same way. Each Main Buy Price and Level is one interval below the previous one. On the graph in Figure 2.3, we have identified five Main Buy Prices and five Levels along with Level 0, one interval above our initial entry price. Level 0 is where we plan to sell our last contract.

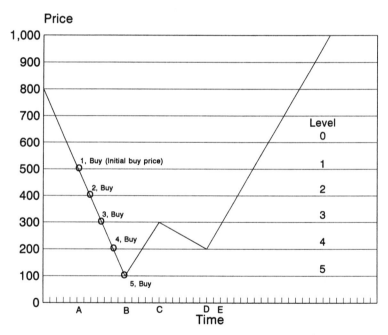

Figure 2.3
The Pretend Market Showing Five Main Buy Prices
and their Levels

29

2.4. The Scale Trading Game Plan

Our scale trading game plan is as follows:

1. As the market drops, we will buy contracts one interval apart at each Main Buy Price.

2. We will plan to sell each contract one interval above its purchase price.

For example, if we buy a contract at Main Buy Price 3 (Level 3), we will sell it for a profit one interval higher in price (Level 2). However, should the market continue to drop, we would buy another contract at Main Buy Price 4 (Level 4) and then plan to sell it one interval higher in price (Level 3).

Note that our game plan consists of buying contracts in a falling market and holding them in inventory with the expectation that fundamental supply/demand forces will adjust sometime in the future resulting in a rising market. We make our profit when we sell them from inventory. When we buy contracts and put them in inventory, we will incur a paper loss on those contracts. This paper loss, called <u>drawdown</u>, is a normal and expected consequence of scale trading.

In this trading strategy, we do not use stoploss orders because we are buying contracts in a falling market and placing them in inventory. Stoploss orders will almost guarantee that we will take a loss on these contracts, which we probably will not be able to recover. This means that we must be well capitalized in order to withstand the drawdown associated with scale trading. We must be both financially and psychologically prepared for this drawdown.

2.5. The Scale Trading Table

At our initial entry point (Buy, 1; Level 1 in Figure 2.3), we know the following information:

1. Our initial entry price, the scale, and the size of the interval.

2. The prices at which we plan to make our subsequent buys should the market drop. This knowledge allows us to place open orders for their purchase. As a result, we don't have to watch the market continually.

3. The price at which each purchased contract will be sold, which will always be one interval higher than the price at which we purchased it. Therefore, we can place an open sell order after we purchase each new contract. Again, we don't have to watch the market continually provided we have a broker who will keep us informed should trades develop during the day. We must, however, review the results at the end of the day and determine if any new buy or sell orders are necessary.

Note that the trading program is almost all mechanical. Once we determine the initial buy price and the size of the interval, scale trading does become entirely mechanical. Those of you who have traded extensively know the value of having a mechanical trading system. It frees you from worry and from the problem of skewed judgment when you have taken a position in the market.

Given the above information, we can make a table called a Scale Trading Table that can guide us as the future unfolds. With this table we are able to calculate the approximate amount of money we will need to see the scale trade through to completion.

Armed with this information, we can then judge whether we have enough money to carry out the scale trade should something go awry. We can calculate the approximate amount of money we may need before making the first buy, but we cannot calculate the actual amount. That you have sufficient capital and reserves is the risk you must be willing and able to take before entering the market. (There is always a risk in commodity trading.)

To complete the table entries, you must know the initial margin requirements and the dollar value of an interval. Let's assume our pretend market has an initial margin requirement of $1,000 per contract. We have previously stated that 1 point in this market is equal to $10. These are values that would be known for a real market before making the first trade.

Table 2.1
The Scale Trading Table
For a Pretend Market

$15,000 + Reserves Recommended

1 Buy Price	2 Holdings to Date	3 Losses to Date	4 Losses per Contract	5 Loss Per Level	6 Paper Losses	7 Required Margin	8 Losses + Margin	9 Sell Price
500	1	0	0	0	0	1,000	1,000	600
400	2	1	1,000	1,000	1,000	2,000	3,000	500
300	3	2	1,000	2,000	3,000	3,000	6,000	400
200	4	3	1,000	3,000	6,000	4,000	10,000	300
100	5	4	1,000	4,000	10,000	5,000	15,000	200

Initial Margin, $1,000; Profit Goal, $1,000 per level

Column 1: Buy Prices. These are the Main Buy Prices, the prices at which we have (or will possibly) purchased contracts. These prices are separated from one another by an interval. These Main buy Prices are marked "Buy" in Figure 2.3.

Column 2: Holdings to Date. These are the number of contracts that we hold in inventory at this Main Buy Price. Our initial purchase in this pretend market is at 500. Therefore, at a price of 500, we hold one contract. At a price of 100, we would hold five contracts in inventory.

Column 3: Losses to Date. This is the number of contracts that have a paper loss. At a price of 500, our initial purchase price for the pretend market, we have one contract in inventory (the one purchased at 500), but it does not have any paper loss. When the price drops to 400, we will have two contracts in inventory. One of these contracts, the one purchased at 500, will have a paper loss. The other contract, the one purchased at 400, will not have any paper loss. By the time the price reaches 100, we will have four contracts with paper losses, and one without any paper loss (the contract purchased at 100).

Column 4: Losses per Contract. In this pretend market each contract will have a paper loss of $1,000 as it drop an interval (from a Main Buy Price to the one below it). Since size of the intervals are the same from top of the scale to the bottom, the amount of paper loss per contract is constant from the top to the bottom.

Column 5: Loss per Level. This is the amount of money we are losing at each level. At a Buy Price of 500, we have no paper loss; therefore, our loss per level is 0. At a Buy Price of 400, we are losing $1,000 per level from the purchase at 500 but nothing yet from the 400 purchase. At a Buy Price of 300, both the contract purchased at 500 and the one purchased at 400 are losing $1,000, but the one purchased at 300 is not yet losing money. Therefore, at a Buy Price of 300, we are losing a total of $2,000. At a Buy Price of 100, we have four contracts losing $1,000 each; therefore, we are losing a total of $4,000 at that level.

Column 6: Paper Losses. This is the drawdown at that Buy Price. It is the sum of all of the contract's paper losses. At a Buy Price of 500, we have no paper losses and at a Buy Price of 400, only the contract purchased at 500 has a paper loss ($1,000). However at a Buy Price of 300, the sum of the paper losses begins to increase at an increasing rate. The contract purchased at 500 has a $2,000 loss and the contract purchased at 400 has a $1,000 paper loss. The contract purchased at 300 has yet to have a paper loss. The sum of these losses ($2,000 + $1,000 + $0) is $3,000. At a buy price of 100, each contract purchased above 100 has a paper loss. These losses are:

Purchased at	Paper Loss
500	$4,000
400	3,000
300	2,000
200	1,000
Sum	$10,000

Column 7: Required Margin. This is the amount of margin needed at each level. The margin for this pretend market is $1,000 per contract. Therefore, for each contract you own, you need $1,000. At Buy Price of 500, you own one contract; your margin requirement is $1,000. At a buy Price of 100, you would own five contracts; Therefore, the margin requirement would be $5,000.

Column 8: Losses + Margin. This is the sum of Columns 6 and 7. This is the most important column in the table because it details your capital requirements.

Column 9: Sell Price. This is the profit-earning price at which you would sell the contract that you purchased at the previous level. For example, at a Buy Price of 500, you plan to sell the contract at 600 for a profit of 100 points ($1,000). Thus, the Sell Price is set at one interval higher than the Buy Price.

2.6. Scale Trading the Pretend Market

Let's assume we are at Point A on the time scale of the chart in Figure 2.4. This identifies Point, 1, the initial buy point. Let's now let our pretend market unfold and see how scale trading works.

A. Buys at the Main Buy Levels

As you can see, as we move from Time A to Time B, the price of our commodity drops. As the market drops, we purchase more contracts, each contract being purchased 100 points (one interval) below the previous one.

The market bottoms at Time B (Point 5; Level 5 in Figure 2.4). At this point in time, we have 5 contracts of the commodity in inventory and a substantial paper loss (drawdown). Much more about drawdown later.

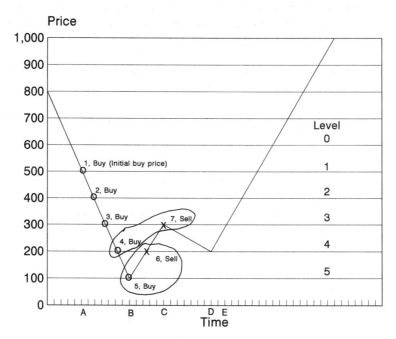

Figure 2.4
The Initial Buys and the First Two Trend
Profits in The Pretend Market

After Time B, the market begins to rally. It moves up to Point 6 (Figure 2.4), at which time we sell the contract we purchased at Point 5 for a 100 point ($1,000) profit. The market continues its rally up to Point 7 (Time C on the time line in Figure 2.4). At this point we sell the contract we purchased at Point 4 for another 100 point ($1,000) profit. (See Figure 2.4.) These two completed trades are circled in Figure 2.4. They are trend profits, a term we will define later in this section.

At Time C we still own three contracts (purchased at Points 1, 2, and 3) and have a 200 point ($2,000) profit. Overall, we still have a drawdown. The three contracts have a total drawdown of $3,000. (How to calculate drawdown will be discussed later.) Subtracting our $2,000 profit from this drawdown figure, we can see that our net drawdown is $1,000.

B. Oscillation Profit

Within a trend, price oscillations occur. The price moves against the prevailing trend for a period of time, then continues in the direction of the trend. Without knowing the future (which we do know in this example), it would appear that at Time C (Figure

34

2.5) the market is making an oscillation against the downtrend. The fact is it actually is an oscillation in an uptrend. We would not recognize this fact in a real market until after Time E (Figure 2.5), the time at which the market:

> 1. Has failed to make a new bottom; that is, reach a price lower than Point 5 (Figure 2.5); and

> 2. Has reached a price that is higher than its previous high, above Point 9 (Level 3) on the chart in Figure 2.5.

   During an oscillation, we sell a contract whenever the price moves up by one interval. As the market price falls, we re-purchase that contract. Consequently, in our pretend market, we re-purchase a contract as the market falls back to Level 4 (Time D, Point 8 in Figure 2.5).

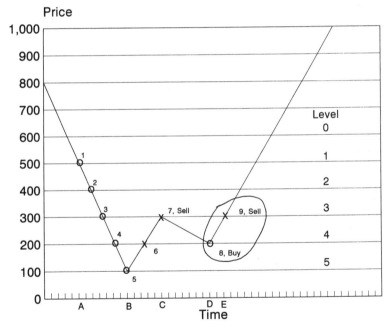

Figure 2.5
The Oscillation Profit

   Had the downtrend remained intact and the market continued to move down, we would have re-purchased another contract at Level 5 also. This would have been confirmation that the downtrend was still intact. However, our pretend market doesn't do that. At Time D (Figure 2.5), it moves upward. As the market moves from Point 8 to

35

Point 9 (Time D to Time E), we sell the contract we just purchased at Point 8. We will sell this contract at Point 9 and collect another 100 points ($1,000) profit. Because this profit occurred as a result of an oscillation, it is called an *oscillation profit*. This profit is identified in Figure 2.5.

C. Trend Profits

Although it was not apparent at the time, the two profits that we took before the oscillation profit (buy at Point 5 and sold at Point 6; buy at Point 4 and sold at Point 7; see Figure 2.4) were trend profits. Trend profits are those taken during an uptrend. As the market continues to rise, we collect three additional profits. These three trend profits are identified in Figure 2.6 with double-headed arrows.

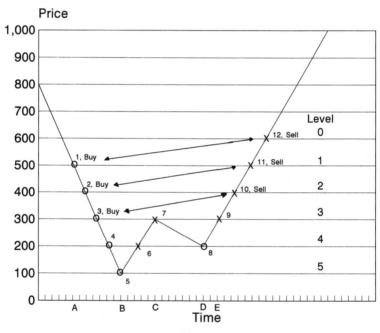

Figure 2.6
Trend Profits after
The Oscillation Profit

Note that the order in which contracts are sold is a first-in-last-out order. Also note, the last sell (Level 0) is 100 points greater than our first buy (Level 1). At Level 0, we have completed the scale trade. The system does not provide any mechanism by which you can buy another contract after Level 0 even if the price of the commodity rises to very high levels. You can, of course, buy another contract at the end of the scale and continue to trade with the trend. But this is not scale trading. This inability to trade above the end of the scale is one of the unfortunate features of classical scale trading.

After we have sold a contract at Level 0, should the price dip below our Initial Buy Point, we can re-establish the scale trade and start over. But this is really a new scale trade and not part of the one we just finished.

D. Percentage Return

A summary of all the buys and sells in our pretend market is in Table 2.2

Table 2.2
Summary of All the Buys and Sells
In the Pretend Market
(See Figures 2.4, 2.5 and 2.6)

Buy Point	Sell Point	Type of Profit	Profit (points)
1	12	trend profit	100
2	11	trend profit	100
3	10	trend profit	100
4	7	trend profit	100
5	6	trend profit	100
8	9	oscillation profit	100
		Total	600 points

For the pretend market, 1 point is equal to $10 (with commissions and fees ignored for simplicity). Therefore, with a total of 600 points profit, our gross profit would be $6,000. The maximum amount of money we would need in our account to make this profit would be the initial margin plus drawdown at Time B (Point 5 in Figure 2.6). To calculate this amount of money, we need the value of the initial margin, which we have set at $1,000 per contract, for this example.

Margin:

  5 contracts at $1,000 per contract = $5,000

Paper loss at Time B:
    Contract 1:   400 points
    Contract 2:   300 points
    Contract 3:   200 points
    Contract 4:   100 points
    Contract 5:   0 points
                  _____
    Total: 1,000 points

  1000 points paper loss at $10 per point = $10,000

Total capital needs at Time B = $5,000 + $10,000 = $15,000

Since our profit in this example was $6,000, our rate of return would be:

$$\frac{\$6,000}{\$15,000} \times 100 = 40\%$$

The rates of return given in this book are not intended to imply you could actually get such a value in the real market. You never would take your account down to zero as would be required for you to obtain the rate of return given here. The value is useful though. It provides a direct comparison of relative efficiencies of the various strategies being presented.

E. Questions

Since the numbers in this pretend market were selected to illustrate the principles of scale trading, it is not surprising that we made a handsome profit. Therefore, two questions come immediately to mind:

   1. "Does it always work this way?"

      Answer: Unfortunately, no.

   2. "Is this percentage return unreasonably high?"

Answer: It is not unreasonably high, provided the contract you are scale trading ends with a substantial up move.

That brings up the next question:

3. "Well, what happens if the market doesn't end with an up move?"

Answer: You have to roll over your contracts into a more distant month and hold them until an upward movement (bull market). This is called a *rollover* and will be covered in more detail later.

2.7. What Futures Can Be Traded Using Scale Trading?

In general, futures markets can be divided into two main groups: (1) financials (interest rates, indices, and currencies) and (2) physical items (grains, livestock, metals, softs, fibers, and energies). This latter group is commonly called *commodities* to distinguish them from the *financial futures*.

With scale trading, we buy contracts in a falling market and sell them in the ensuing up market. We are counting upon the downtrend to be followed by an uptrend -- that the Bear market will be followed immediately by a Bull market. With commodities, this is not an unreasonable expectation. With financials, it is considerably more iffy. The prices of financial futures are not necessarily controlled by the laws of supply and demand, but often by governments, politicians, and their bureaucrats. Therefore, in scale trading <u>We Only Trade Commodities</u>.

2.8. What Commodities Can We Trade Using Scale Trading?

Many different commodities are offered on the exchanges. Not all of them have sufficient volume (lots of contracts that are traded each day) to be suitable for trading. Low-volume commodities may be suitable for a producer who deals in the physical item, but not for the trader who does not wish to receive or deliver the physical item. Traders need volume -- they need the ability to quickly buy and sell their contracts. Also, markets with small volumes have a wide price range between the bid and ask price on the market floor. A market order (an order requiring an immediate buy or sell) can get a very bad fill (a poor price or a price unrelated to the current quoted price). In considering a possible scale trade, we suggest you only initially consider the commodities listed in Table 2.3.

Within these 23 basic commodities, you will find several different contract sizes and types, as well as different exchanges that offer contracts. Space precludes an in-depth coverage of the pros and cons of one type of contract or exchange over another. Consult with your broker on the suitability of any specific commodity or commodity contract prior to starting a scale trading program.

Table 2.3
Commodities Suitable for Scale Trading

Grains	Energies
Wheat	Crude Oil
Corn	Heating Oil
Oats	Unleaded Gasoline
Soybeans	Natural Gas
Soybean Oil	
Soybean Meal	
Livestock and Meats	**Metals**
Live Cattle	Gold
Feeder Cattle	Silver
Lean Hogs	Platinum
Pork Bellies	Copper
Softs and Fibers	
Cotton	
Cocoa	
Coffee	
Sugar	
Orange Juice	

2.9. Short Scale Trading

When you take a short position, you first sell a contract then buy it back at a later date. With a short position, you will make a profit if the price goes down and lose money if the price goes up. (See Figure 2.7.)

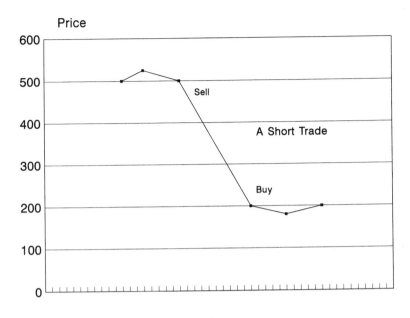

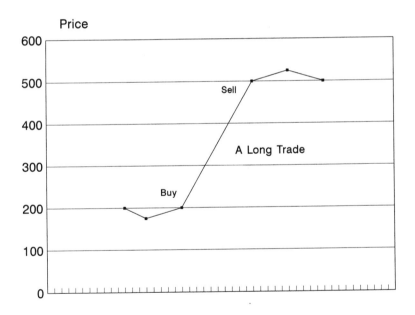

Figure 2.7
A Short and a Long Trade

When you take a long position, you do just the reverse. You first buy the contract and then sell it at a later date. With a long position, you will make a profit if the price goes up and lose money if the price goes down. (See Figure 2.7.)

In theory, you can short scale trade just as easily as you can long scale trade. In a short scale trade, your sell levels would be tiered up. As the price rises, you would sell (go short) a contract at each level. When prices reach a top and begin to descend, you would buy the contracts back for a profit. (See Figure 2.8.)

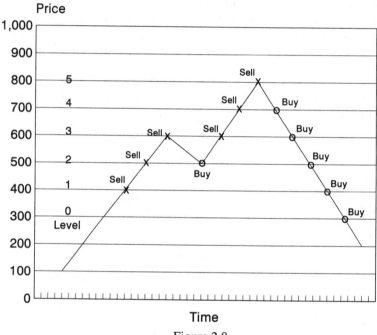

Figure 2.8
A Short Scale Trade

While in theory this strategy should work, we find in the real world it is extremely dangerous.

A. How High is Up?

In times of true scarcity, there is no ceiling to how high a commodity price can rise. This means that your potential drawdown could be gigantic -- in the hundreds of thousands of dollars, if not larger.

This is not an unjustified fear. Consider the case of September Coffee in 1994. Prices rose to $1.20, which at the time seemed very high. Had you started a short scale trade at $1.24 on about 5/17/94 and used an interval of 5¢ (equal to $1,875), you would have accumulated 31 contracts by the time it topped at $2.74 on 7/13/94. Your paper loss on these contracts alone (not including any margin requirement) would have exceeded $870,000. That is a pretty hefty drawdown for even the most well-heeled trader. Short scale trading such a market is not conducive to restful nights nor peaceful weekends. The problem with short scale trading is that you cannot say where or when its top is likely to be formed.

However, with long scale trading you need a bottom. You are buying contracts in a falling market relying on the concept that a bottom will occur in the not too distant future. This is much more likely to occur than seeing a top form during times of true scarcity. We have discussed the reasons why in Chapter 1, "The Scale Trading Family."

We Never Short Scale Trade. The risk is unlimited. We always long scale trade. Our risk is more predictable, but unfortunately, not entirely predictable. When we use the term scale trade, we mean long scale trade (Figure 2.9).

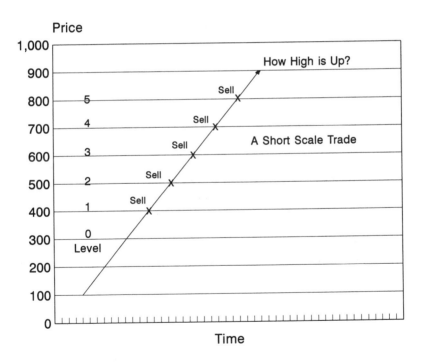

43

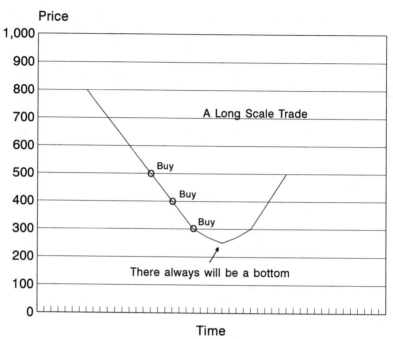

Figure 2.9
Don't Short Scale Trade

2.10. Starting a Scale Trade

Assuming that the price is low enough (see below), start scale trading a specific contract month three to six months before its expiration date as long as it has sufficient volume that your order can be quickly filled. If the volume is too small, there will be a large range between the bid and ask prices on the floor of the exchange. When this is the case, you will probably get a poor price if you place a market order or attempt to have a stop order executed. In these cases, you should use limit orders. In any case, this is a problem you should discuss with your broker.

A. At What Price Do You Begin Scale Trading?

Scale trading depends upon prices dropping, the market forming a bottom, and then prices rising and recovering in an uptrend. If you start trading at too high a price, you will purchase an excessive number of contracts on the way down. This will result in a hefty drawdown of your account. In fact, the drawdown can be large enough that it will exceed the value of your account and force you into liquidation. This means a true financial loss. Drawdown is a paper loss unless you have to liquidate. Because drawdown can result in true financial loss, we will discuss it in detail later in this chapter.

One way to control drawdown is to not start your scale too high. Be sure your initial price is low enough that it is in reasonable range of a possible bottom. The question, of course, is, "How to do that?"

The rule of thumb that scale traders use is, "Never start a scale trade at a price that is greater than one-third of a multiple year range". In many cases, this price may still be too high. However, the one-third value gives you a starting price from which you can begin to consider the possibility of a scale trade.

B. Calculation of the One-Third Price of a 15-Year Range

Surprisingly, there is no generally accepted method to make the calculation of a one-third value for a multiple year price range. There are several different ways it can be done. Not surprisingly, however, is that they all give approximately the same value. We will present one technique to make the calculation. The procedure that we will present gives a perfectly reasonable value so that you can make additional evaluations.

Assume that you are considering a scale trade in Wheat. What is the price that defines the lower one-third of a multiple year range? To make the calculation, you need a perpetual weekly or monthly high-low chart for the commodity you wish to trade. Such charts are provided by several vendors and are called *Long Term Charts*. A 15-year monthly high-low chart of Wheat is given in Figure 2.10.

We want to delete any prices that are aberrations (spikes) from our calculations. Our goal is to obtain the prices where the market has made major tops and bottoms over the years. A simple way to do this is to select the four highest and four lowest values from the chart, discard the highest high and the lowest low, and average the remaining three highs and then the three lows. This gives us a computed high and low from which we can make the one-third calculation.

Figure 2.10
Monthly Fifteen Year High-Low
Chart of Wheat

C. Calculation of the Computed High and Low For Wheat

From Figure 2.10 we find the following four highs.

1996	717
1996	527
1989	449
1997	442

Delete the 1996 price of 717 from the list and average the other three highs by adding them together and dividing by 3.

Computed high = (527 + 449 + 442)/3 = 473

For the computed low, we select the four lowest values.

$$
\begin{array}{ll}
1985 & 241 \\
1991 & 244 \\
1987 & 248 \\
1993 & 277
\end{array}
$$

Discard the 1985 value of 241 and average the remaining three lows, again by adding them together and dividing by 3.

$$\text{Computed low} = (244 + 248 + 277)/3 = 256$$

D. Calculation of the 1998 One-Third Value for December Wheat.

The difference in these two prices is:

$$473 - 256 = 217$$

One-third this difference is:

$$\frac{217}{3} = 72$$

Add the one-third value to the computed low:

$$256 + 72 = 328$$

The one-third computed price is approximate; therefore, round it to a working value.

328 is rounded to a working value of 330.
(This value means a price of $3.30 for a bushel of Wheat.)

The one-third value for Wheat in 1998 is 330. A scale trading purist would say, "Begin scale trading at any price under 330." A more conservative scale trader would say "Let's wait until the price gets lower than that value before we begin." Who is right? No one knows what the future holds. But if the purist starts at a higher price and has sufficient capital and the tenacity to hold on for a long time if things go awry, then he or she will make more money than the conservative trader who starts at a lower price. What is a sufficient amount of capital? That brings up the thorny issues of Rollovers and Drawdown, which we will discuss shortly.

E. Deciding on a Scale Size

An interval of one-half of the initial margin value has been recommended for classical scale trading. For Wheat, the initial margin requirement on 7/7/98 was $675 (see Table 2.7). Therefore, this recommendation would give an interval of approximately 7¢ ($350), where 1¢ = $50.

Wheat can make a down move of 80¢ to 100¢ ($1.00) after it crosses into its lower one-third range. Using a down move of 100¢ ($1.00), a 7¢ interval would require 15 levels (15 contracts deep). (There would be 15 contracts, not 14 as simple division would imply. The additional contract comes from the fact you have one contract at each end.) If you use such a small interval, you must be prepared for a large capital requirement (margin and drawdown). How large? Using 7/7/98 initial margin value, and the fact that 1¢ of Wheat equals $50, your capital requirements would be slightly over $46,875 if a 100 point drop occurred. (Calculations of margin and drawdown are covered in Section 13 and 14 of this chapter.)

By using such a small scale you would indeed capture almost all of the oscillation profits. There is no way to calculate or estimate how many there might be. However, assuming that there were none, you can at least expect to make 15 trades of $350 each, or $5250, in trend profits. This is about an 11% return on your investment, not a lot of return for the risk you would be taking.

There are some alternatives that would need smaller amounts of capital and can yield a much higher rate of return.

(1) **Use a larger scale.** Consider using a larger interval. For example, use an interval equal to the initial margin requirement. This would be about 13¢ ($650) and would require 8 levels to cover a 100¢ ($1.00) in price. Your capital requirements for this size of a interval would be $23,600. Your trend profit would be the same (8 x $650 = $5,200); therefore, your percentage return is larger (22%).

A larger interval gives even a higher percentage return. By using the daily limit of Wheat as the interval ($1,000, 20¢), a 100¢ ($1.00) drop in the price would require 6 contracts and $19,050 in capital for margin and drawdown. Trend profits would be $6,000, but for comparison's sake, let use $5,200 for the trend profit. This latter value would be a 27% return.

The moral here is that, unless you can capture an awful lot of oscillation profits, a bigger interval is better.

48

(2). **Use another member of the Scale Trading Family.** Interval Scale Trading[SM] and **ParaScale Trading**[SM] do not have the capital requirements that classical scale trading does. These alternate trading methods capture both the trend profits and most of the oscillations. They are described in detail in chapters that follow.

2.11. Ending a Scale Trade

Nothing goes on forever. Even scale trades must come to an end. You terminate a classical scale trade when you sell the last contract in your inventory. This is the first one you bought. You sell it at Level 0, one interval above its purchase price.

This is one of the more frustrating problems with scale trading. After experiencing a substantial drawdown, and maybe one or two rollovers, you finally clear your inventory and sell your last contract. And then, you watch the market take off -- it climbs into the stratosphere. It's enough to give you the hiccups.

2.12. Rollovers

If you scale trade for very long, there will be a time when your contract month approaches its first notice day (the day on which, and after, delivery is possible) and you will be forced to sell your contract(s). If the price of the commodity is above your entry price, but still below your next sell level, then you don't have a problem. Just sell the contracts and terminate the scale trade. However, that's rarely the case. The usual circumstance is that all of your contracts will be below your purchase price and you will have to take a real loss. These are real losses. They are to be tallied in your win-loss record as a loss. At year end (tax time) these losses are to be deducted from your profits. There are some folks who claim these aren't real losses because they have only rolled them over and these are "just in inventory". They tout a phenomenal win-loss record, as much as 22 years without a losing trade. I bet they sing a different tune at year-end tax time.

When you have sold your losing contracts, you will be faced with a choice:

1. Accept your loss; or
2. Rollover your contract into a more distant month.

Accept your losses. If your loss is small (and only you can judge that), the best advice is to just accept the loss as part of the commodity business and continue with another, but new, scale trade.

Rollover. If , however, you judge your losses too large to ignore, then you can roll your contracts into a more distant month. This requires taking new positions in a contract month whose first day notice is far into the future. For example, if you have contracts in July Wheat, you would sell your July contracts and purchase December Wheat.

In carrying out the rollover, you would not simply enter a market order to sell July Wheat and another market order to buy December Wheat. Market orders require the floor broker to execute the order at whatever price he or she can get when the order is received. Consequently, you can get very bad prices by just placing a market order. A far better technique is to enter a *spread order*. A spread order means that both the sell and the buy are executed at the same time and at a price difference, called the *basis*, specified in the order. Be sure to discuss the spread order with your broker in order to determine a reasonable basis before you enter it.

You rollover the same number of contracts as you sell. In classical scale trading, the purchases are made in the new contracts at the same time the old ones are sold. Upon rollover of your contracts you have the choice of continuing the scale trade in the new contract month, or terminating it after the rollover contracts have been sold.

We will first show you how to calculate the prices at which you should sell your new contracts so that you can both recover your losses and gain the profit you had planned to make. Then, we will discuss some additional features of the rollover such as what to do if you can't sell all of your new contracts at your rollover target price.

A. Rollover Calculations

To explain the rollover calculation, we are going to assume the following about our pretend market:

> **Example 1.** After Time C, we were forced to liquidate our remaining 3 contracts at a price of 250 because first notice day was imminent. (See Figure 2.11.) At liquidation, our losses were 3 contracts and a total of 450 points. We immediately purchased 3 new contracts using a spread order in a distant month at a price of 350. Since our buy price (350) was greater than our sell price, the market can be identified as a *normal carrying charge market* (see Section 2.12E).

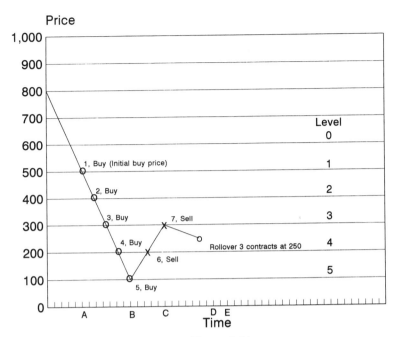

Figure 2.11
Pretend Market for
Rollover Example 1

We fill out a Rollover Table to make the rollover calculations. The Rollover Table for Example 1 is Table 2.4. This is the same table as described by Wiest in his book, "You Can't Lose Trading Commodities", but simplified here for easier calculations.

Table 2.4
Rollover Table for Example 1
Pretend Market with Three Losses

Scale Entry Price	Close Out Price	Gain <Loss>	Original Profit Goal	Rollover Value	New Entry Price	New Sell Price
500	250	<250>	100	350	350	700
400	250	<150>	100	250	350	600
300	250	<50>	100	150	350	500

The first column in Table 2.4 (Scale Entry Price) is the price at which we purchased the contracts. In our example, these are the first three contracts purchased at 500, 400, and 300.

51

The second column (Close Out Price) is the price at which we sold each of the contracts. In our example, we sold each at 250.

The third column (Gain or <Loss>) is the number of points we gained or lost on each contract. This, of course, is the difference between our purchase and sell price. If the value is a loss, then we enclose it in brackets (< >) to signify that it will be treated as a negative number in the calculations. Profits are positive numbers and are not enclosed in brackets. In Example 1 all values are losses, therefore a negative number enclosed in brackets.

The fourth column (Original Profit Goal) is the profit we had planned to make on the contract when we first purchased it. In our pretend market, we had planned on a profit of 100 points for each contract.

The fifth column is the Rollover Value. This is the number of points we will add to the rollover purchase price, the price of the new contract, to obtain the target sell price for that contract. The Rollover Value is calculated using the following formula.

Rollover Value = (Original Profit Goal) - (Profit or <Loss>)

This formula is a little tricky to use because it involves the subtraction of either a positive or a negative number, depending upon whether you had a profit or a loss. In this first example, all three contracts had losses; therefore, we will need to subtract negative numbers. In our next example, Example 2, we will modify the numbers so that one of them is positive (a profit).

In algebra, subtraction of a negative number means "change the sign and add." Therefore, let's go through this table, row by row, to ensure that you understand how the Rollover Value is calculated.

Row 1:

Rollover Value = (Original Profit Goal) - (Profit or <Loss>)
= 100 points - (-250 points)
= 100 + 250
= 350

As you can see, when we subtract the -250, we actually are adding +250. If you find this confusing, just remember--if you had a loss then add the loss to your original profit goal. This is logical because you have to make up the loss along with making the original goal.

<u>Row 2:</u>

$$
\begin{aligned}
\text{Rollover Value} &= (\text{Original Profit Goal}) - (\text{Profit or <Loss>}) \\
&= \quad 100 \text{ points} \quad - \quad (-150 \text{ points}) \\
&= \quad 100 \quad\quad\quad + \quad 150 \\
&= \quad 250
\end{aligned}
$$

<u>Row 3:</u>

$$
\begin{aligned}
\text{Rollover Value} &= (\text{Original Profit Goal}) - (\text{Profit or <Loss>}) \\
&= \quad 100 \text{ points} \quad - \quad (-50 \text{ points}) \\
&= \quad 100 \quad\quad\quad + \quad 50 \\
&= \quad 150
\end{aligned}
$$

The sixth column (New Entry Price) is the price at which we purchased our new contract. In Example 1, this price was given to be 350 for each rollover contract.

The seventh column, and last column (New Sell Price), is the price at which we will sell each of the rollover contracts. This target price is the sum of the new entry price (Column 6) and the Rollover Value (Column 5). We may or may not be able to sell all of these rollover contracts at these prices, but this is what we would like to do.

Note that the total "profit" we would realize from the sale of the three rollover contracts at our target prices is 750 points. This "profit" would re-coup our 450 point loss and provide us with the 300 points profit we originally wanted.

Before discussing some details of rollover, let's use another example in which we have both a profit and losses when we were forced to liquidate.

Example 2. We are forced to liquidate our remaining 3 contracts at a price of 350. Therefore, at liquidation, we have 2 contracts that have losses, and 1 contract with a profit. Let's assume that our re-entry price in the new contract is 210. As in our previous example, the rollover was executed using a spread order. Since the buy price (210) is less than the sell price (350), this market can be identified as an *inverted market* (see Section 2.12E).

The Rollover Table for this example is Table 2.5.

Table 2.5
Rollover Table For Example 2
Pretend Market with Both Profit and Loss

Scale Entry Price	Close Out Price	Gain <Loss>	Original Profit Goal	Rollover Value	New Entry Price	New Sell Price
500	350	<150>	100	250	210	460
400	350	<50>	100	150	210	360
300	350	50	100	50	210	260

53

There are two differences between this example and the first one: (1) the contract purchased at 300 shows a profit, and (2), the re-entry price in the new contract is considerably lower.

Rows 1 and 2 both show losses in column 3, the Profit <Loss> column. The calculation of the Rollover Value for these two rows uses the same procedure as was shown for Example 1. We will not repeat it here.

The calculation of the Rollover Value for Row 3 is different because we have a positive value (a profit) in Column 3. The calculation is as follows

Row 3:

Rollover Value = (Original Profit Goal) - (Profit or <Loss>)
= 100 points - (+50 points)
= 100 - 50
= 50

Subtraction of a positive number is straightforward arithmetic operation. Here, it is logical because we don't need 100 points to reach our original profit objective (100 points) for this contract. We received 50 points when we were forced to liquidate. Therefore, we only need 50 more points upon rollover.

Again, note that in Example 2 the total "profit" we would gain by selling all of the rollover contracts at their target price (450 points) is equal to our losses (150 points) plus our desired profit (300 points).

The fact that we were able to buy the new contracts in this example at a price less than the close out price of the old contracts did not affect the calculation. Regardless of the new rollover price, all we have to do is to add the Rollover Value to the new purchase price.

B. Another Method for Rolling Over Contracts

There is an alternate method for rolling over contracts. It is described in Chapter 3, "**Interval Scale Trading**[SM]". The alternate method uses an averaging approach to the calculation of the sell price of the rollover. Some scale traders find it superior to the classical method described here.

C. What to Do When You Cannot Sell All of Your Rollover Contracts?

You have to rollover the contract(s) again. Sell the first rollover contract(s) and buy new ones in a more distant month. Let's continue with our example in the Pretend Market and expand Example 1 to include a second rollover.

> **Example 3.** (A Continuation of Example 1.) After rollover, we were able to sell the lower two contracts at our target sell price. However, the market never rose to 700. As a result we could not sell the last contract. (See Table 2.4.) As the new first notice day approached, we were forced to sell our last contract at a price of 550. We immediately purchased one contract in a distant month at 600.

As you can see, one contract did not make its sell goal. Therefore, we rollover only one contract for the second rollover. As before, we construct a Rollover Table (Table 2.6).

Table 2.6
Rollover Table for Example 3
of the Pretend Market

Scale Entry Price	Close Out Price	Gain <Loss>	Original Profit Goal	Rollover Value	New Entry Price	New Sell Price
350	550	200	350	150	600	750

In our example, the rolled-over contract showed a profit (200 points) from its purchase price of 350. This profit is subtracted from the original rollover goal of 350 points to obtained the new Rollover Value of 150 points. This value is then added to the most recent purchase price (600) to obtain our new sell price of 750.

In classical scale trading, this rollover procedure is continued until we get our desired price. Once that is attained, we will have recovered our drawdown and our original profit goal.

D. Do You Continue with The Scale Trade in The Rollover Contract?

After you purchase the rollover contracts, you may wish to continue the scale trade should the market continue down. To do this you would construct a new scale trading table like the one shown in Table 2.1. One feature you should consider, however, is to widen the scale to spread out the total of the Rollover Values within the scale trade. In that way the burden of the drawdown and "missing profit" is distributed over several contracts rather than just a few.

E. Rolling Into Inverted and Carrying Charge Markets

An *inverted market* is one in which the prices of the more distant months are below the prices of the current months. Inverted markets imply a current scarcity. They occur commonly in a rising, or bull, market. A *carrying charge market,* or *normal market* is one in which the price of the current months is less than that of the distant months. A carrying charge market implies the current supply is adequate. A carrying charge market is commonly observed in a falling, or bear, market. The price differential reflects the cost of carrying the supply (interest, storage, and insurance costs) into the future.

Inverted Market. With an inverted market, you would be rolling into a more distant month at a price below your liquidation price. In general, this should not cause a problem. No special precautions need be considered.

Carrying Charge Market. With a carrying charge market, you would be rolling into a more distant month at a price higher than your liquidation price. This can cause a problem, particularly if a bear market is underway. In a rollover, you are counting on an upward move to recover your drawdown and "lost" profit. There may not be enough upside potential for this to occur.

Wiest, in his book "You Can't Lose Trading Commodities", recommends dropping a few contracts in this circumstance and taking a real loss. That is certainly one possibility. Another possibility is to use another rollover procedure, such as the one discussed in Chapter 3, "**Interval Scale Trading**^{SM}".

2.13. Capital Requirements: Margin

Margin is the deposit that is required by the exchange when a commodity futures contract is bought or sold. The broker's commission house makes this deposit for you. They in turn want your money in an account with them before they do business with you.

The amount of money needed for margin can be in T-Bills drawing interest for you as long as the T-Bills are on deposit in the broker's commission house.

There are two different types of margin requirements -- initial margin requirement and maintenance margin requirement. When you first buy a commodity contract, your account must have a value at least equal to the *initial margin requirement* for that commodity. Once you have purchased a contract, you must maintain an account value equal to or greater than the *maintenance margin requirement* for that commodity contract.

For the computation of capital requirement of a scale trade, we use the initial, rather than the maintenance, margin requirement. Therefore, we will ignore maintenance margin in the following discussion.

A. What Your Margin Requirements Depend Upon

The amount of margin that is required depends upon:

1. The commodity itself;
2. The number of contracts of the commodity in your inventory.

Volatility. The volatility of a commodity's price is the major determining factor in the margin size. The more volatile the commodity, the greater is its margin. Oats, for example, usually a non-volatile commodity, had an initial margin requirement of $540 on 7/7/98. Soybeans, a far more volatile commodity, had an initial margin requirement of $1350 on the same date. Because price volatility can change without warning, all margin requirements are subject to change without notice. Consequently, all quoted margin values must also be dated.

Number of Contracts Held. Margin requirements are quoted in dollars per contract. Therefore, the required margin amount equals the number of contracts of that commodity times its initial margin requirement. For example, if you own 10 contracts of a commodity, then your requirements for that commodity will be 10 times the quoted initial margin requirement for that commodity.

We need to discuss margin calculations before going to the all important subject of drawdown. Interwoven throughout all of our discussions in this section and the one that follows will be two related calculations. (1) "What is our current margin requirement and/or drawdown?", and (2) "What would be our margin requirement and/or drawdown if the commodity moves against us?". This latter question is the most important one because it allows us to plan our money management.

B. Calculations of Margin Requirements

When you purchase a commodity contract you must have the amount of money equal to, or greater than, the <u>initial</u> margin requirement in your account. After you have made your purchase, you must maintain that amount of money in your account at all times. Some typical initial margin requirements as of 7/7/98 are listed in Table 2.7.

Table 2.7
Selected Initial Margin
Requirements as of 7/7/98

Commodity	Initial
Wheat	$675
Live Cattle	$608
Silver	$2,025
Cotton	$998
Crude Oil	$2,025

A sample calculation will illustrate the key principles of margin requirements.

Example. You have a scale trade of Wheat with 5 contracts in inventory. You are contemplating the purchase of a 6th contract.

(a). What is your margin requirement for the 5 contracts?

Using Table 2.7, we see that the margin requirement for 1 contract of Wheat is $675. Therefore, with 5 contracts our total margin requirement for Wheat is (5 x $675) or $3375.

(b). What is your margin requirement at the time you purchase the 6th contract of Wheat?

Again using Table 2.7, the margin requirement for Wheat is $675. Therefore, the margin requirement for 6 contracts is:

Margin requirement for Wheat = (6 x $675) = $4050

2.14 . Capital Requirements: Drawdown

Drawdown is the amount of money deducted from your account due to price erosion of a commodity contract you own. Drawdown reduces the value of your account. If drawdown decreases your account value below its maintenance margin requirements (called a *debit balance*), you will be issued a *margin call*, a request for more money. A margin call will force you to add money to your account or to liquidate contracts.

Drawdown is a paper loss. A *paper loss* is the amount of money that your account value has decreased because a contract you own has decreased in price. Since you still own the contract, your account value can still go up or down depending on what the future holds. In contrast to a paper loss, a *real loss* is the amount of money that your account value has decreased by a contract that you no longer own. To recover a real loss, you must re-enter the market--that is, take a new commodity position with all its inherent risk. We do not tally paper losses in our win-lose record, but we do tally our real losses.

Real loss results from a margin call that causes liquidation. A margin call, in turn, is triggered by a decrease in account value below the sum of its margin requirements. The decrease in account value occurs because of drawdown. As you can see, the true culprit of a real loss is drawdown, even though drawdown itself is only a paper loss. All scale traders' money management decisions revolve around drawdown or potential drawdown.

If you, as the scale trader, have correctly estimated drawdown, you will make a substantial amount of money. If you can stick with it, you are almost guaranteed to **Be A Winner Trading Commodities**™. That is, it is guaranteed as much as anything can be guaranteed in the commodity business.

If you, as the scale trader, miscalculate drawdown and underestimate the amount of capital needed, you will lose money. Indeed, if you quit, or if you are undercapitalized, you will lose very large sums of money. (Not paper losses, but real money.)

If you are going to scale trade, you must master the technique for calculating drawdown. You must make these calculations before entering a scale trade. Armed with drawdown projections, knowledge of your financial situation, and a thorough understanding of your psychological make-up, you can make the decision whether to scale trade a commodity or not.

Because of its importance for the successful scale trade, we will discuss drawdown in detail. Therefore, we will divide the subject into three subtopics:

1. How to calculate drawdown for any price below the current market
   price;
2. What controls drawdown; and
3. How to minimize drawdown.

A. How to Calculate Potential Drawdown

Drawdown at any point in time is the sum of all your paper losses. Let's use our pretend market to first show how drawdown is calculated using a long-hand, laborious method of calculation. Then, we will present a general formula for its calculation. Finally we will apply the formula to a real market.

Drawdown = Sum of all Paper Losses

B. Calculation of Drawdown for the First Three Levels of the Pretend Market

Recall that we said a 100 point move in the pretend market is equivalent to $1,000 ($10 per point). Since we set the levels 100 points apart, each level down from the level where we bought a contract is a paper loss of $1,000 for that contract. (Our emphasis here will be on calculating the current drawdown, not projecting it.)

Drawdown At Point 1, Level 1 of the Pretend Market

Our initial buy is at Point 1. Because the market has not yet gone down from there, we have no paper loss. Therefore, our drawdown is $0. (Don't confuse drawdown with your total capital needs. The latter also includes margin. At Point 1 in the pretend market, even though our drawdown is $0, we do need at least $1,000 for the initial margin. In this section of the chapter, however, we are only discussing drawdown--that portion of the capital needs resulting from price erosion.)

Drawdown At Point 2, Level 2 of the Pretend Market

Contract 1. Since the market has gone from Level 1 to Level 2, the initial contract (Contract 1) has a paper loss of one level. Because in the pretend market we set this value at $1,000, the paper loss for Contract 1 is $1,000.

Contract 2. At Level 2, the second contract does not have a paper loss.

Total Drawdown: Sum of the Paper losses = $1,000 + $0
                                             = $1,000

Drawdown At Point 3, Level 3 of The Pretend Market

At Level 3, we have three contracts, but only two have a paper loss.

Contract 1. At Level 3, we have a paper loss of two levels. Since each level is equivalent to $1,000, the paper loss for Contract 1 is $2,000.

Contract 2. In going from Level 2 to Level 3, we have a paper loss of one level for Contract 2. Again, since one level is equivalent to $1,000, our paper loss for Contract 2 is $1,000.

Contract 3. Since we are at Level 3, we have no paper loss for Contract 3.

Total drawdown: Sum of the paper losses = $2,000 + $1,000 + $0
                                           = $3,000

C. General Formula and Table for Calculating Drawdown

It is quite laborious to calculate the potential drawdown in the way we have been doing it. It is especially laborious when the level number is large, like 20 or 50. It is far simpler, and will be quite instructive, to use a formula calculation. Furthermore, a formula allows us to calculate projected drawdown -- a must for proper money management. Our emphasis will now shift from calculating current drawdown to projecting it.

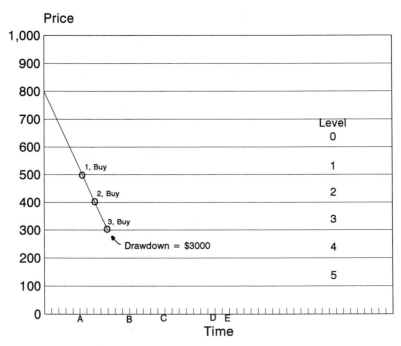

Figure 2.12
Drawdown for Point 3, Level 3
of the Pretend Market

The calculation for the paper loss requires two formulas. The first is the calculation of the multiplier for that level. This formula assumes the levels have an equal space between them (an equal dollar value from one level to the next) and that a purchase is made at each level, except for Level 0. The formula for this calculation is:

$$\text{Multiplier for the Level} = \frac{(\text{level number})^2 - (\text{level number})}{2}$$

For those of you who hate algebraic formulas, the following table to Level 20 is provided.

Table 2.8
Multiplier for The Levels

Level Number	Multiplier		Level Number	Multiplier
1	0		11	55
2	1		12	66
3	3		13	78
4	6		14	91
5	10		15	105
6	15		16	120
7	21		17	136
8	28		18	153
9	36		19	171
10	45		20	190

The second formula calculates the total paper loss for that level assuming the price is still at that level. This formula requires the dollar value for the difference between levels. In our example, we set the interval (the difference between any two levels) to 100 points to a value of $1,000.

Total paper loss = (Multiplier for the level) x (Dollar value of a level)

In our example, our paper loss per level is $1,000. At Level 3, the multiplier for Level 3 is 3 (see Table 2.8). Our paper loss is, therefore, $3,000. At Level 5, the multiplier for Level 5 is 10 (again, see Table 2.8); therefore, our paper loss would be $10,000.

D. Drawdown is Exponential

Drawdown (paper loss) is exponential, not linear. (See Figure 2.13). This can be a serious problem if it is not recognized. When you are at Level 4, the multiplier for the paper loss is 6 times the interval. If we double the number of contracts by going to Level 8, the multiplier is 28 times (not 8 nor 12, as you might have guessed). At level 16, it is 120 times the interval and at Level 32 it is 496 times the interval. Any scale trade that goes down more than 5 levels (5 levels deep) is fraught with danger. It is the scale trader's failure to recognize the exponential character of the paper loss component of drawdown that leads to rack and ruin.

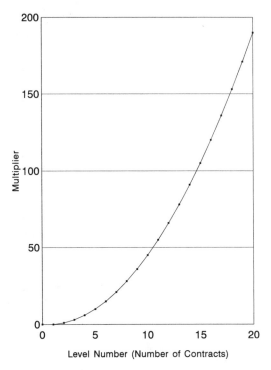

Figure 2.13
Drawdown is Exponential

E. What Controls Drawdown?

Three things control drawdown:

> 1. The market itself;
> 2. How low in the downtrend you start with your first contract; and
> 3. The size of the interval.

64

The <u>first component</u> is the market itself. You have absolutely no control over it. If the market drops from your first entry point, you can't make it go up. No one can. Furthermore, you can't accurately calculate how far it might drop. No one can. You can make an educated guess of how far it might drop or where the bottom might be. But an educated guess is still a guess. There truly is no way to calculate the bottom. The best you can do when you take your initial position is to make an educated guess as to the market's bottom, have adequate money in your account in case you are wrong, and hope for the best.

The <u>second component</u> is the price at which you start trading the downtrend phase of the market. You do have control over this component. You decide where you start scale trading. The closer you can start to the bottom, the smaller will be your drawdown. In classical scale trading, you start your trading program when the prices penetrate into the lower one-third of a multiple year range. For some, this may still be too high. However, with classical scale trading, you must take positions in the down phase in order to take profits in the ensuing up phase. Therefore, you must experience drawdown before you can make a profit. This is psychologically difficult to do, but it is a necessity. This aspect of scale trading is not a major problem with the other members of the Scale Trading Family.

The <u>third component</u> is the interval of the scale. While you have no control over market action, you do have direct control over the size of the interval. In this respect, it is like the initial entry point. The basic rule is:

The larger the interval -- The smaller the drawdown

For example, with our pretend market, if we use an interval of 100 points ($1,000) our drawdown to the low point was 5 contracts and $10,000. If we had used 200 points ($2,000), at the same low point our drawdown would have been 3 contracts and $6000. This is a reduction of 40%. In fact, the rule of thumb is:

Doubling the size of the interval decreases drawdown by about 40%.

F. A Real Market Example

Let's take a real market example to emphasize this point. Let's assume we want to scale trade Wheat starting at $3.30. Let's also assume we estimate that the bottom will be $2.50. With a 10¢ interval between Main Buy Points, our scale down to $2.50 would require 9 levels. (Not 8 as you might think; see Table 2.9.)

Table 2.9
The Nine Levels of Wheat
using a 10¢ Interval

Level	Wheat Price
1	3.30
2	3.20
3	3.10
4	3.00
5	2.90
6	2.80
7	2.70
8	2.60
9	2.50

At Level 9, our drawdown would be:

10¢ in Wheat is equal to $500.
The multiplier at Level 9 is 36 (see Table 2.8).
Therefore, our paper loss would be:
    36 x $500 = $18,000

Total Drawdown = $18,000

We also need money in the account to cover margin. For these calculations, we use the initial margin requirement. We do this for a little added insurance. The initial margin for Wheat on 7/7/98 was $675 (see Table 2.7). Therefore, 9 contracts would take 9 x $675 or $6,075.

Our total capital requirement for a 9 level, 10-cent scale trade of Wheat would be:

Total Capital Requirement = Margin + Drawdown
    = $6,075 + $18,000
    = $24,075

Let's now see what happens if we increase the interval size to 20¢. The trades with 20¢ interval are given in Table 2.10.

Table 2.10
The Five Levels of Wheat
Using a 20¢ Interval

Level	Wheat Price
1	3.30
2	3.10
3	2.90
4	2.70
5	2.50

At Level 5, our drawdown would be:

An interval of 20¢ would equal $1,000.
The multiplier at level 5 is 10 (See Table 2.8).
Therefore, the paper loss is:
10 x $1,000 = $10,000

Total Drawdown = $10,000

For margin on 5 contracts we would need 5 x $675 = $3,375.

Consequently the total capital requirement would be:

Total Capital Requirement = Margin + Drawdown
= $3,375 + $10,000
= $13,375

Percent Reduction in Drawdown by Using a Larger Interval. If the market drops from $3.30 to $2.50 and if you use a 20¢ interval rather than a 10¢ interval, your drawdown will be 43% less (rounded).

$$\frac{(\$24,075 - \$13,750)}{\$24,075} \times 100 = 43\%$$

Do You Lose Trend Profits By Using A Larger Interval? But you might say, "If I use a smaller interval, I will make more money!" Not true, provided you consider only trend profits. The trend profit is the same for both scales. (See Table 2.11.) In addition, as you can see in Table 2.11 your percentage return is higher if you use a larger interval.

Table 2.11
Comparison of Profits Using
a 10¢ and a 20¢ Interval

10¢ Interval				20¢ Interval		
Buy	Sell	Profit		Buy	Sell	Profit
330	340	10		330	340*	10
320	330	10		310	330	20
310	320	10		290	310	20
300	310	10		270	290	20
290	300	10		250	270	20
280	290	10				
270	280	10				
260	270	10				
250	260	10				
		90				90
	Total:	($4,500)			Total:	($4,500)
Capital required:		$24,075		Capital required:		$13,750
Percentage return:		19%		Percentage return:		33%

*The top of the 20-cent scale was set to 340 to allow for an equal comparison.

There is, however, a significant difference in the two scales. With the smaller interval, you will get more oscillation profits. How many more depends on the market and cannot be predicted. Obviously, a compromise is needed.

G. How to minimize drawdown

As we have said, drawdown is the bane of scale trading. It is deceptively dangerous because it is exponential. You can't control or predict the market. Therefore, the only way to control drawdown is by starting lower in the down phase of the market and/or by using a larger interval. These two principal ways to minimize drawdown are the bases of the other members of the Scale Trading Family, for example, **Interval Scale Trading**[SM] and **ParaScale Trading**[SM].

1. Use a very large interval.
This method of scale trading is called **Interval Scale Trading**[SM] and was invented by this author. It is detailed in his book The

Intelligent Speculator (McGraw Hill Professional Publishing, 1333 Burr Ridge Parkway, Burr Ridge, IL 60521). This method is designed to capture both trend and oscillation profits while using a very large interval to reduce drawdown. Its new and enhanced version is the subject of Chapter 3 of this book.

2. **Do not take a position in the market until there is some evidence that a bottom is in place**.
   This method of scale trading is called **ParaScale Trading**[SM] and was invented by Laurence J. Pagano. The Beacon Companies, Inc. may be contacted for more details of this system. (The Beacon Companies, Inc., P.O. Box 770883, Naples, FL. 34107; 1-888-232-2668). It is the subject of Chapter 4 of this book.

2.15. Practical Problems with Classical Scale Trading

There are a number of very practical problems with classical scale trading as it was presented by Wiest in his book "You Can't Lose Trading Commodities". Many of these problems have already been mentioned in this chapter, but will be revisited here for completeness. Some of these problems cannot be corrected because they are inherent in the nature of the scale trading technique itself.

The principal problems are:

1. Capital requirements;
2. Psychological requirements of the trader;
3. Rollover strategy; and
4. Missing out on the big bull runs.

A. Capital Requirements

You cannot trade using the classical scale trading system with a tight budget. Wiest mentions the need for $50,000 to scale trade five different commodities. Under some market conditions, $50,000 would be more than adequate. Under other market conditions, however, it is not enough. It all depends upon the overall commodity market. When all markets are in downtrends, scale traders can expect to experience maximum drawdown and a lot of rollovers. The overall direction of the commodity markets is reflected in the direction of the CRB (Commodity Research Bureau) Index. When it is in a major downtrend, scale traders can expect a lot of trouble. This has been the case in the mid 1980's and in 1997-1998.

Drawdown is exponential. The more levels you buy going down a scale, the greater your drawdown is at each level. Drawdown increases at an increasing rate. Drawdown becomes extremely painful after five levels down. A lot of scale traders have been very badly hurt by the combination of scaling too many commodities and a general bear market in all commodity prices. When you are one or two contracts deep in several different commodity scales, you should not experience any financial problems. When those scales slip to five to seven contracts deep, you may suddenly discover you do have a problem. Because drawdown is exponential, you could suddenly discover you have a major problem and have to liquidate contracts. There is no technique in classical scale trading to "cut your losses short." Once you are buried in contracts, no matter what you do, it will be extremely painful. The only solution is to avoid it by anticipating that it might occur and planning your scale trade accordingly.

Interval Scale Trading^{SM} and **ParaScale Trading**^{SM} address the problem by reducing the drawdown. The actual mechanics of how these two system work will be described in their respective chapters in this book.

B. Psychology of the Scale Trader

For go-go speculators, scale trading is borrrrrrring. They want action. They want to buy. They want to sell. They want to call their broker. They want to feel the pulse of the market. Scale trading for these traders is so boring, they want to play with it. And when they do, they lose money.

On the flip side of the coin, scale trading for sedate investors is terrifying. They watch their account value drop like a rock during the drawdown phase. They finally reach their breaking point, panic, and quit. They then, of course, lose everything. The sad part of it is, their breaking point is invariably the market bottom. Had they stuck with it, they would have made money.

If you are a go-go trader looking for a new hot trading system or a sedate investor trying to get a higher rate of return than a T-Bill, don't scale trade. It is almost guaranteed you will lose money.

Scale trading is a conservative form of commodity trading. In order to scale trade, you have to be well capitalized and use your money wisely. You have to understand what you are trying to do, how to do it, and have an iron will to see it through.

Wiest entitled one of his chapters "Patience is a Virtue." In scale trading, that's the truth. If you are patient, well capitalized, disciplined, and don't tinker with the system, you will be handsomely rewarded for your efforts. If you are not, or cannot, then don't be surprised if you lose money. For some individuals, having someone else skilled in scale trading manage their money may be the best course of action.

C. Rollover Strategy

Classical rollover strategy as described by Wiest leaves much to be desired. In his chapter on rollovers, Wiest dismisses the subject with the following statement:

> "When I began this chapter I wondered if I really needed to include it in the book. I have so little necessity for employment of rollovers during the years I have scale traded that I thought the subject could probably be omitted, but I included it to mitigate your fears if you are concerned about holding a large number of expiring contracts."

This has not been the experience of large numbers of traders. They have found rollovers to be an integral part of scale trading. The method described by Wiest, and re-verbalized in this chapter, probably is not the best approach to rollovers. It involves buying a potentially large number of contracts in a falling market immediately after selling your expiring contracts.

Interval Scale Trading[SM] and **ParaScale Trading**[SM] have less of a rollover problem than classical scale trading, but both do employ rollovers. However, they use a completely different approach than that described for classical scale trading.

D. Missing Out on the Big Bull Runs

Last, but not least, is the extremely exasperating experience of selling your final classical scale trading contract only to watch the market take off and rise beyond your wildest dreams. There is no method in classical scale trading to take advantage of these major runs.

Chapter 3

Interval Scale Trading^{SM}

3.1. Introduction

Interval Scale Trading^{SM} is classical scale trading with several enhancements. These enhancements are designed to:

1. Reduce drawdown;
2. Capture both trend and oscillation profits above and below the initial purchase; and
3. Provide an improved rollover procedure.

Before proceeding with a detailed description of the mechanics of **Interval Scale Trading**^{SM}, let's revisit some of the advantages and disadvantages of classical scale trading.

In the <u>advantages column</u>, it is a mechanical system that matches the three aspects of a commodity market that you can predict: that the market will always have a bottom, that the market will trend, and that the market will have oscillations. Classical scale trading is a rather simple system that doesn't require constant monitoring of the market, nor does it require a computer for calculations. The buys and sells are identified before the fact so open orders can be entered. It is a system that doesn't use stop loss orders (which can be viewed as either an advantage or disadvantage depending upon your temperament).

In the <u>disadvantages column</u>, it is a capital intensive system. Long positions must be purchased in a falling market and the contracts placed in inventory before they can be sold for a profit. The scale trader must be willing and able to weather large drawdowns of his or her account without undue distress. It employs a rollover method that can force the trader to purchase a large number of contracts during an unfavorable market situation. Its design prevents the trader from taking advantage of the big bull moves for which commodities are famous.

However, the real and unrelenting problem of classical scale trading is drawdown. Drawdown is exponential. Drawdown increases at an increasing rate the deeper you go into a scale. Any classical scale trade that goes more than 5 levels deep is fraught with danger.

As we discussed in Chapter 2, there are two methods to reduce drawdown in scale trading. One method is to take the initial position as low as possible in the down phase of the market. The scale trading system that employs this technique is called **ParaScale**

Trading^{SM}, and is discussed in Chapter 4. Another method to reduce drawdown is to use a very large interval. This is the technique used in **Interval Scale Trading**^{SM} and is discussed in this chapter.

As was mentioned in Chapter 2, **Interval Scale Trading**^{SM} was invented by this author and has been published in his book <u>The Intelligent Speculator</u> (McGraw Hill Professional Publishing, 1333 Burr Ridge Parkway, Burr Ridge IL 60521). The descriptions that follow are enhancements of that system.

3.2. Two Pretend Markets to Explain Interval Scale Trading^{SM}

As discussed in Chapter 2, the larger the interval, the smaller the drawdown. Doubling the size of the interval reduces drawdown by about 40% (see Section 2.13E). However, you just can't use a very large scale with classical scale trading because oscillation profits will be lost. Oscillation profits can provide a significant portion of the profit in scale trading.

Interval Scale Trading^{SM} solves this dilemma by using two scales--one for the down phase of the market and another for the up phase. This chapter contains two variations of **Interval Scale Trading**^{SM} -- one using a sell-buy technique and another without the sell-buy. We need to discuss the variation using the sell-buy first in order to see why the second variation works as it does. The second variation is discussed in Section 3.11. It is the combination of **ParaScale Trading**^{SM} with **Interval Scale Trading**^{SM} without the sell-buy that provides one of the more powerful scale trading methods, however, and this is discussed in Chapter 4.

As we did with classical scale trading, we are going to use a pretend market to explain the principles of **Interval Scale Trading**^{SM}. However, it will be necessary to use two different pretend markets for a complete explanation. The first of these pretend markets is the same one we used to explain classical scale trading. It has an oscillation in the up phase of the market. The second pretend market we will use in this chapter has an oscillation in the down phase of the market. An oscillation in the down phase does not alter the mechanics of classical scale trade, but it does alter those of **Interval Scale Trading**^{SM}.

3.3. Pretend Market 1. An Oscillation in the Up Phase of the Market

The basic principle behind **Interval Scale Trading**^{SM} is to use a large interval in the down phase of the market, then switch to a smaller interval as the market goes into its up phase. A large interval reduces the drawdown during the down phase and the smaller interval allows for the capture of oscillation profits.

Let's look at the first pretend market we are going to use for our initial explanation and summarize what would happen if this market were classically scale traded using an interval of 100 points (Figure 3.1). This is identical to what we did in Chapter 2. (See Section 2.6 for a complete discussion.)

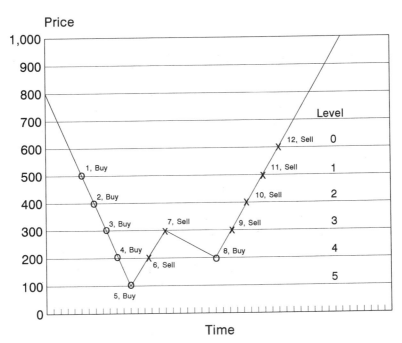

Figure 3.1
Classical Scale Trading.
Pretend Market 1
Using an Interval of 100 points

A summary of the result of this trading is given in Table 3.1. As we did in Chapter 2, we will use 1 point = $10 and a margin requirement of $1,000 per contract.

Table 3.1
Classical Scale Trading.
Pretend Market 1.
Using an Interval Size of 100 points

Number of contracts at market bottom:	5
Margin:	
five contracts at $1,000 each	$5,000
Drawdown:	
One level is equal to $1,000	
At Level 5, the multiplier is 10	
10 x $1,000 per level	$10,000
Total capital requirements:	
$5,000 + $10,000	$15,000
Profit:	
5 Trend profits at $1,000 each = $5,000	
1 Oscillation profit at $1,000 each = $1,000	
Total:	
$5,000 + $1,000	$6,000
Rate of return:	
($6,000/$15,000) x 100	40%

Now let's consider what would happen if we double the size of the interval (see Figure 3.2). The results are summarized in Table 3.2. As you can see, we purchased only three contracts during the down phase and sold three contracts during the up phase. But we missed the oscillation profit completely. When the interval size is too large, we can completely miss oscillation profits.

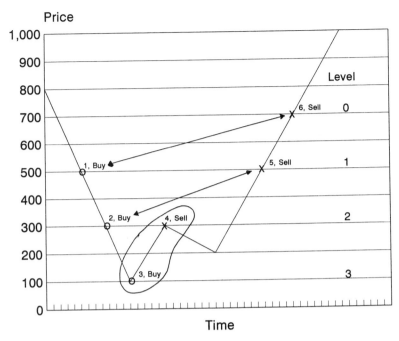

Figure 3.2
Classical Scale Trading Pretend Market 1
Doubling the Interval Size to 200 points

Inspection of Tables 3.1 and 3.2 shows that doubling the interval to 200 points:

1. Requires only 3 versus 5 contracts to reach the market bottom;

2. Misses the oscillation profit;

3. Reduces drawdown by 40%; and

   [($15,000-$6,000)/$15,000] x   100 = 40%

4. Increases our rate of return from 40% to 67%.

Item 2 is not reflected in the profit comparison nor in comparison of the two rates of return. One of the differences between the two trades is the placement of Level 0. In the 100-interval trade, the last sell was at 600 while in the 200-interval trade the last sell was at 800. If we take our last sell at 600 for both classical scale trades, the difference becomes more apparent. The comparison is summarized in Table 3.3.

Table 3.2
Classical Scale Trading.
Pretend Market 1.
Doubling the Interval Size to 200 points

Number of contracts at market bottom:	3
Margin: three contracts at $1,000 each	$3,000

Drawdown:
   One level is equal to $2,000
   At Level 3, the multiplier is 3
   3 x $2,000 per level
	$6,000

Total capital requirements: $3,000 + $6,000	$9,000

Profit:
   3 Trend profits at $2,000 each = $6,000
   0 Oscillation profit at $1,000 each = $0
      Total:
      $6,000 + $0
	$6,000

Rate of return: ($6,000/$9,000) x 100	67%

Table 3.3
Classical Scale Trading.
Pretend Market 1 with the Last Sell at the Same Price (600)
versus Interval Size

	Interval Size		
	100 Points		200 Points
Total Profit:	600 ($6,000)		500 ($5,000)
Rate of Return	40%		55%

Let's now show the results of **Interval Scale Trading**[SM] this market without yet explaining how it is carried out. (We will devote much of this chapter to its explanation.) The trading is shown in Figure 3.3 and the summary of the results is given in Table 3.4.

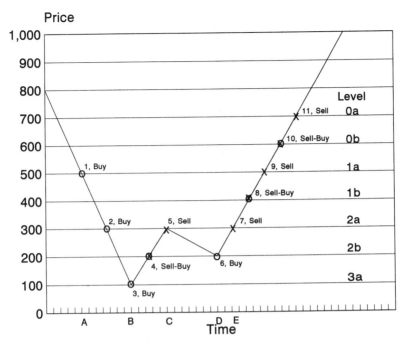

Figure 3.3
Interval Scale Trading[SM] of
Pretend Market 1

In comparing these **Interval Scale Trading**[SM] results with those of the classical scale trades just given, a number of things stand out.

1. The drawdown picture is very similar to that of the 200-point classically scaled market:
   a. Only 3 contracts were required to reach the market bottom; and
   b. There was a 40% reduction in drawdown and in total capital required compared to the 100-point classical scale trade.

2. The profit picture is very similar to the 100-point classically traded market:
   a. All trend profits were obtained;
   b. The oscillation profit was not missed; and
   c. The rate of return was 78% (The last contract was sold at 700; see Figure 3.3).

79

Table 3.4
Summary of **Interval Scale Trading**^{SM}
of Pretend Market 1

Number of contracts at market bottom:	3
Margin:	
three contracts at $1,000 each	$3,000
Drawdown:	
One level is equal to $2,000	
At Level 3, the multiplier is 3	
3 x $2,000 per level	$6,000
Total capital requirements:	
$3,000 + $6,000	$9,000
Profit:	
6 Trend profits at $1,000 each = $6,000	
1 Oscillation profit at $1,000 each = $1,000	
Total: $6,000 + $1,000	$7,000
Rate of return:	
($7,000/$9,000) x 100	78%

What we see is that **Interval Scale Trading**^{SM} has garnered the best of both of the classical scale trades yet did not inherit any of the worst features. Let's now see how the **Interval Scale Trading**^{SM} can be carried out.

3.4. Initial Steps in Interval Scale Trading^{SM}

The initial steps in **Interval Scale Trading**^{SM} are similar to those in a classical scale trade.

1. Select the price to begin the trading program;
2. Select the main interval;
3. Calculate the intermediate interval; and
4. Identify the Main Buy Prices, the Intermediate Prices, and their respective levels.

A. Select the Price to begin the Interval Scale Trading^{SM} Program

As we did in Chapter 2, we are going to select the price marked "1. Buy" as our starting price for Pretend Market 1. This point is marked on the graph in Figure 3.3. The actual technique used to determine the starting price in a real market is the same as that used in classical scale trading. (See Sections 2.10A and B and also Section 3.9A.).

B. Selection of the Main Interval and the Intermediate Interval

In our example of classical scale trading in Chapter 2, we used an interval of 100 points. For **Interval Scale Trading^{SM}**, we are going to use a main interval of 200 points. In general, we select a value that is twice the interval used in a classical scale trade. Recommendations for the main interval of selected commodities are given in Table 3.12, in Section 3.9B.

Once the main interval is selected, we use that value to calculate the intermediate interval. The intermediate interval is set at one half of the main interval. Therefore, our intermediate interval is really the same size as that used in classical scale trading.

> **Intermediate Interval = (Main Interval) /2**

C. Identify the Main Buy Prices and Intermediate Buy Prices

For Pretend Market 1, the main buy prices will be at 700, 500, 300, and 100. The initial buy price is at 500 and the last sell will be at 700. The intermediate buy prices are half-way between the main buy prices and are located at 600, 400 and 200 in this pretend market. Table 3.5 shows the relationship of the main and intermediate buy prices.

We also need to identify the buy prices by a level number. To keep the main and intermediate levels separate and easily identified we will use an "a" or "b" designation after the level number. An "a" designation means that it is a main level and a "b" means it is an intermediate level. Therefore, Levels 0a, 1a, 2a, and 3a are the main levels and Levels 0b, 1b and 2b are the intermediate levels. Since we number the levels from the top to bottom, the intermediate levels are always at a price below their main levels. Table 3.5 also shows how the levels are labeled according to this convention.

Table 3.5
Main and Intermediate Buy Prices
and Levels for Pretend Market 1

Main	Intermediate	Level Number
700	--	0a
--	600	0b
500	--	1a
--	400	1b
300	--	2a
--	200	2b
100	--	3a

3.5. Interval Scale Trading^{SM} Game Plan

We can only give a partial description of the **Interval Scale Trading**^{SM} game plan at this time. We need the explanation of Pretend Market 2 for a full description.

For the moment, the following will suffice:

1. In a declining market, we buy at the main levels.
2. In a rising market, we sell and then immediately buy at the intermediate levels.
3. In a rising market, we only sell (not buy) at the main levels.

This game plan uses the sell-buy technique, which as we have stated is no longer recommended. However, we do need to understand how it works in order to understand **Interval Scale Trading**^{SM} without the sell-buy.

3.6. Interval Scale Trading^{SM} Pretend Market 1

A. Buys at the Main Buy Levels

Let's assume we are at Time A on the time scale of Figure 3.4. This identifies the initial buy point, "1, Buy."

As we move from Time A to Time B (Figure 3.4), the price of the commodity drops. As the market drops, we purchase more contracts but only at the main buy levels (Levels 2a and 3a). We do not purchase contracts at the intermediate buy levels (1b and 2b).

The market bottoms at Time B. (In a real market, of course, we would not know we were at the bottom.) This is the level at which we have maximum capital requirements for the trade. Let's pause and compare the capital requirements for **Interval Scale Trading**[SM] with those of classical scale trading (100 point interval) at maximum drawdown. (Table 3.6).

Table 3.6
Comparison of Maximum Drawdowns
of Classical Scale Trading and **Interval
Scale Trading**[SM]

	Classical Scale Trading	**Interval Scale Trading**[SM]
Number of contracts:	5	3
Margin requirement:	$5,000	$3,000
Drawdown:	$10,000	$6,000
Total capital requirement:	$15,000	$9,000
	Percentage reduction:	40%

B. The Sell-Buy

As the market moves from Time B towards Time C (Figure 3.4), prices move up to Level 2b, a price of 200. At Level 2b, we sell the contract we purchased at Buy Point 3 (Level 3a) for a 100 point profit ($1,000). We immediately buy another contract at 200.

These transactions -- the selling of one contract for a profit and the immediate purchase of another contract at the same price,-- are called a *sell-buy*. (Section 3.11 describes **Interval Scale Trading**[SM] without this sell-buy. The results of **Interval Scale Trading**[SM] with or without a sell-buy are identical.)

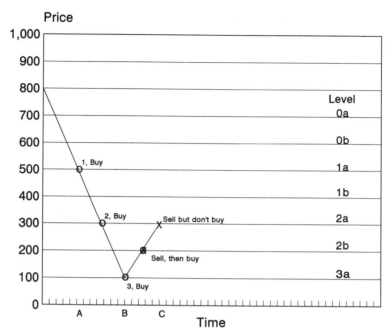

Figure 3.4
Interval Scale Trading^{SM} to Time C
in Pretend Market 1

Pretend Market 1 continues from Level 2b (a price of 200) up to Level 2a (a price of 300) (Figure 3.4). At Level 2a we sell the contract we purchased at Level 2b (the purchase of the sell-buy) for another profit of 100 points ($1,000). We do not make a new purchase at this level because we already have a contract at Level 2a, which is the one we purchased during the down phase of the market. (See Figure 3.4.)

C. Oscillation Profit

In moving from Time C to Time E (Figure 3.5), both classical scale trading (100 point interval) and **Interval Scale Trading**^{SM} have the same market action. As the market drops to 200 (Time D; Level 2b in Figure 3.5) we buy a new contract. When the market rises to 300 (Time E in Figure 3.5), this new contract is sold for a 100 point profit ($1,000). This is the oscillation profit that nets $1,000 for both systems.

Again, let's pause and compare the results of the two systems after the oscillation profit (Table 3.7). As you can see, if we consider only drawdown, **Interval Scale Trading**^{SM} is $1,000 in the black while classical scale trading is at break even.

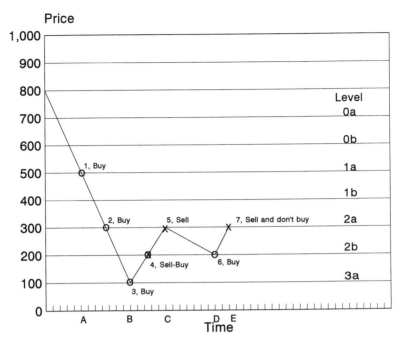

Figure 3.5
Interval Scale Trading[SM]
Pretend Market 1 to Time E.
The Oscillation Profit

Classical scale trading has $3,000 in actual drawdown and $3,000 in profit to offset that paper loss. **Interval Scale Trading**[SM] has $2,000 in actual drawdown and $3,000 in profit. This is generally how it works. **Interval Scale Trading**[SM] is ahead of classical scale trading during the scale trade. However, they will become equal in profits at the end of the scale trade.

D. Trend Profits After The Oscillation Profit

After the oscillation profit (after Time E in Figure 3.5), both classical scale trading and **Interval Scale Trading**^{SM} take 3 trend profits of 100 points each (a total of $3,000). (See Figures 3.6 and 3.7).

Table 3.7

Comparison of Classical Scale Trading and
Interval Scale Trading^{SM} **at Time E**
of Pretend Market 1
(See Figure 3.5)

	Classical Scale Trading	Interval Scale Trading™
Number of contracts:	3	2
Margin requirement:	$3,000	$2,000
Drawdown:	$3,000	$2,000
Number of profits	3	3
Trend profits:	$2,000	$2,000
Oscillation profits:	$1,000	$1,000
Total profits:	$3,000	$3,000
Capital needs excluding margin:	0	+$1,000

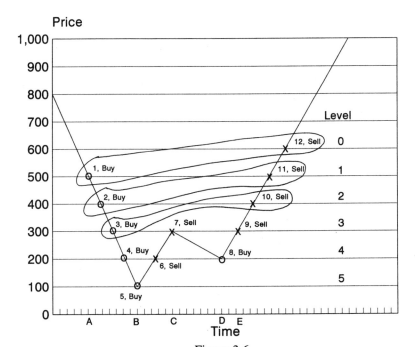

Figure 3.6
Classical Scale Trading
The Three Trend Profits after the Oscillation Profit
are Circled.

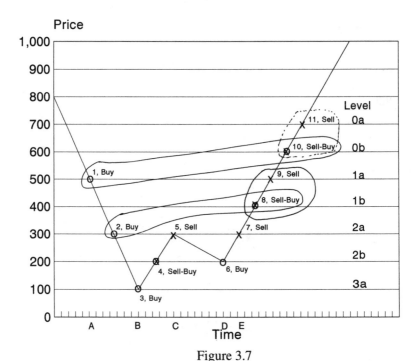

Figure 3.7
Interval Scale Trading[SM] .
The Three Trend Profits after the Oscillation Profit
are Circled. (A Fourth Possible Profit is Marked with
a Dotted Circle.)

E. Total Profit from the Trade

With both trading systems we reach Level 0 (Level 0b for **Interval Scale Trading**[SM]) with $6,000 profit and 6 round turn commissions (6 buys and sells). Note that the sell-buy technique does not increase the number of commissions when compared with classical scale trading. Had we continued **Interval Scale Trading**[SM] to the end of its scale, (Level 0a) our profit would have been $7,000.

F. Trading Above the Initial Buy

At Level 0, classical scale trading ends. There is no mechanism to remain in the market should a major bull market develop. This aspect of classical scale trading is extremely frustrating. **Interval Scale Trading**[SM] does have a mechanism to trade above the initial buy -- the sell-buy. At Level 0a, should the market conditions warrant, we can sell-buy (rather than just sell) and remain in the market.

88

G. Rate of Return from the Interval Scale Trading[SM]

Table 3.8 gives a summary of the buys and sells in Pretend Market 1 for **Interval Scale Trading**[SM]. For simplicity, it is assumed that the sell-buy occurred at the same price. This will not be the case in a real market. In Table 3.8, **Interval Scale Trading**[SM] is shown to continue to Level 0a, yielding 700 points profit. Had the scale trade stopped at Level 0b, there would have been 600 points profit.

Table 3.8
Interval Scale Trading[SM.]
A Summary of All Buys and Sells
for Pretend Market 1
(See Figure 3.3 or 3.7)

Buy Point	Sell Point	Type of Profit	Profit
1	10	Trend profit	100
2	8	Trend profit	100
3	4	Trend profit	100
4	5	Trend profit	100
6	7	Oscillation profit	100
8	9	Trend profit	100
10	11	Trend profit	100
		Total:	700

For the pretend markets, 1 point is equal to $10 (with commissions and fees ignored for simplicity). Therefore, the gross profit of 700 points would be $7,000. The total amount of money we would need to make this profit includes the initial margin for 3 contracts plus their drawdown at Time B (Figure 3.3 or 3.7). As before, we use a margin of $1,000 for the pretend markets.

Table 3.9
Interval Scale Trading^{SM}
Summary of Results from
Pretend Market 1 to Level 0a
(A Gross Profit of $7,000)

```
Margin:
        Three contracts at $1,000 per contract  =  $3,000

Paper loss at Time B:
        Contract 1:   400 points
        Contract 2:   200 points
        Contract 3:     0 points
                    --------------
        Total:        600 points

        600 points at $10  per point  =  $6,000

Total capital needs at Time B:
                        $3,000  +  $6,000  =  $9,000

                    ($7,000)
Rate of Return:     ----------  x  100  =  78%
                    ($9,000)
```

H. Questions

Since the numbers in the pretend market were selected to illustrate the principles of **Interval Scale Trading^{SM}**, it is not surprising that the rate of return was high.

1. "Does it always work out this way?"

    Answer: Unfortunately, no.

2. Is the rate of return unreasonably high?"

    Answer: Yes and no. A more reasonable value would be in the range of 40%, provided, of course, the contract ended in a substantial up move. However, the real market examples given at the end of this book show a much higher rate of return.

3. "If the contract doesn't end with a substantial up move, is it necessary to rollover into a more distant contract?"

Answer: Yes. The rollover procedure for **Interval Scale Trading**^{SM} is different from that for classical scale trading. It will be discussed in Section 3.11.

4. "It seems to me that the sell-buy is a waste of commission money. Why not just hold the contract and sell it at a higher price rather than sell it half-way there and then buy another one?"

> *Answer*: It is true that a sell-buy wastes commission money. The sell-buy is a mechanism to take partial profits from the market yet remain in the market. A second use of the sell-buy is to keep us in the market above the initial entry point. The third use of the sell-buy is to provide us with a logical plan to trade the market.
>
> Because in a mathematical sense, addition and subtraction are both independent of the order in which they are carried out, the buys and sells can be arranged in different orders and yield the same profit (or loss) as that of **Interval Scale Trading**^{SM} (see Section 3.11). However, the different orders are not necessarily logical in the eyes of a Commodity Trader. **Interval Scale Trading**^{SM} does present a logical sequence of events that can be followed by a Trader as the future commodity price action unfolds. The price you pay for this logical sequence of events is a few extra commissions.
>
> For those of you who find the use of a sell-buy objectionable, there is an alternate way to carry out **Interval Scale Trading**^{SM}. It doesn't use the sell-buy and doesn't look the same as the **Interval Scale Trading**^{SM} presented here even though it is based upon it. However, the overall financial results of **Interval Scale Trading**^{SM} with and without the sell-buy are identical. This alternate trading method is presented in Section 3.11, **"Interval Scale Trading**^{SM} Without the Sell-Buy"**.

3.7. Pretend Market 2: An Oscillation in the Down Phase of the Market

The pretend market that we have been using does not cover the situation where the oscillation profit is taken during the down phase of the market. With classical scale trading, an oscillation profit in this location does not present any unique problems. As the market moves up during an oscillation, we sell contracts for a profit. As the market rolls over and continues down, we buy an additional contract at each lower level.

The technique for the calculation of the drawdown for a classically scale traded market with an oscillation in its down phase is the same as before (Section 2.14), except that the oscillation profits are subtracted from the maximum drawdown value. (See Table 3.10.)

Figure 3.8 shows the buys and sells using classical scale trading (100 point interval) for Pretend Market 2 to the point of maximum drawdown at Time D. The results at maximum drawdown are summarized in Table 3.10

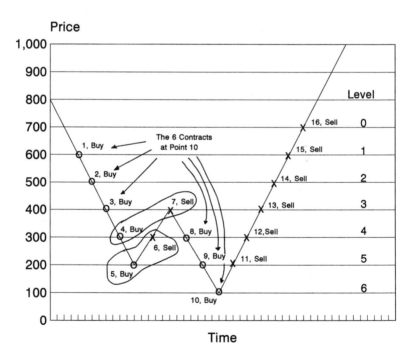

Figure 3.8
Classical Scale Trading.
Pretend Market 2 with Oscillation Profits in the
Down Phase of the Market Circled

92

Table 3.10
Classical Scale Trading.
Capital Requirements of Pretend Market 2
to Market Bottom

Number of contracts:	6
Initial margin requirement: 6 x $1,000	$6,000
Drawdown: Multiplier at Level 6 is 15 15 x $1,000 per contract	$15,000
Capital needs to Level 6: $6,000 + $15,000	$21,000
Less Profit from oscillations: 2 Oscillations at $1,000 each	-$2,000
Total capital needs to Time D: $21,000 - $2,000	$19,000

With **Interval Scale Trading**^{SM}, an oscillation in the down phase of the market (see Figure 3.9) does present two problems that need to be discussed.

1. The calculation of drawdown; and
2. How to re-establish the large interval on the way down.

A. Calculation of Drawdown with an Oscillation in the Down Phase of the Market

The formula method for the calculation of drawdown at the market bottom is not valid for **Interval Scale Trading**^{SM} when there are oscillations in the down phase of the market. The formula requires an equal dollar difference between contract buys (between levels). Once we sell-buy at an intermediate level, this requirement is no longer met. Therefore, the formula method of calculation cannot be used.

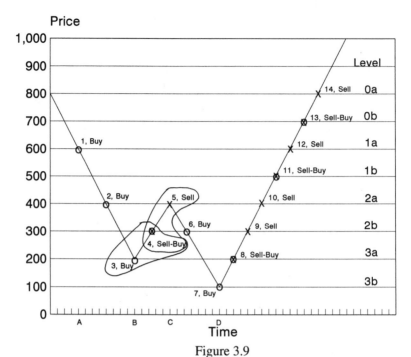

Figure 3.9
Interval Scale Trading[SM] of Pretend Market 2.
Market Bottom at Time D and Oscillation Profits Circled

Consequently, what we are going to do is: (1) present a method for calculating drawdown to a current market price; and (2) present another method that will provide a range of drawdown values. We use the first method to see where we are in terms of current capital needs and the second to estimate our potential capital needs in the future at a price below the current market.

Calculating Current Drawdown. At current time, we know the number of contracts we own, the number of oscillations, and the price at which we want to calculate the drawdown (current price).

Our calculation, shown in Table 3.11, involves subtraction of the current price from the purchased price of each contract to obtain the drawdown in points for that contract. We sum the individual drawdown, convert the total drawdown to dollars, and then add the margin requirement. Finally, we subtract the oscillation profit to obtain the capital needs at the current price.

Example: At Time D in the **Interval Scale Trading**^{SM} of Pretend Market 2 (Figure 3.9), we own 4 contracts, which were purchased at 600, 400, 300, and 100. The current price is 100 and our total oscillation profit is 200 points. (We will continue to use 1 point = $10 and an initial margin value of $1,000 per contract.) What is our capital need at Time D?

The calculation is shown in Table 3.11.

Table 3.11
Interval Scale Trading^{SM}
Calculation of Capital Needs at Time D
in Pretend Market 2

Number of contracts:	4
Initial margin requirement:	
4 x $1,000	$4,000
Drawdown	
Contract 1 (purchased at Level 1a) (600 - 100) = 500 points	
Contract 2 (purchased at Level 2a) (400 - 100) = 300 points	
Contract 3 (purchased at Level 2b) (300 - 100) = 200 points	
Contract 4 (purchased at Level 3b) (100 - 100) = 0 points	

Total: 1,000 points	
1,000 points at $10 per point	$10,000
Maximum capital needs to Level 3b (Time D, Figure 3.9)	
$4,000 + $10,000	$14,000
Less Oscillation profits:	
2 Oscillation profits at $1,000 each	-$2,000
Total capital needs at Time D:	
$14,000 - $2,000	$12,000

Calculation of Projected Drawdown. We can't calculate projected drawdown accurately without knowing how many oscillations there will be. And that is something we can't predict. However, we can calculate a range of drawdown values.

To illustrate the calculation of a range of drawdown values, consider the following example:

Example. Calculate the range of drawdown values and capital required for **Interval Scale Trading**[SM] of the following market.

> Initial purchase: 700
> Main Interval: 200 points
> Intermediate Interval: 100 points
> Point Value: 1 points = $10
> Initial Margin Requirement: $1,000 per contract
> Projection of price to: 100

At one end of the range is the case where the market has no oscillation. The formula presented in Section 2.14C is valid in this case because all purchases are made at major intervals and each level is equidistant from the next. The calculation is identical to that made for Pretend Market 1 (Section 3.6) and is repeated below for completeness. An example of such a market is given in Figure 3.10.

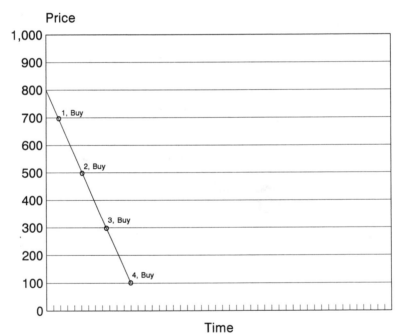

Figure 3.10
Interval Scale Trading[SM]
A Pretend Market with
No Oscillations

Calculation Assuming No Oscillations (See Figure 3.10.)

Levels to a price of 100: 4	
Multiplier at Level 4 (see Table 2.9): 6	
Drawdown to Level 4:	
6 x $2,000	$12,000
Contracts at Level 4: 4	
Initial margin requirement:	
4 x $1,000	$4,000
Capital requirement	
$12,000 + $4,000	$16,000

At the other end of the range is a market that forces us to buy a contract at every main and intermediate level. An example of such a market is given in Figure 3.11. In this case **Interval Scale Trading**^{SM} collapses to a classical scale trade and again the formula is valid because the purchases are equal dollar value distant from each other (each one-half interval apart).

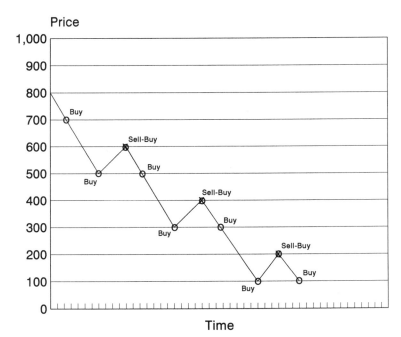

Figure 3.11
Interval Scale Trading^{SM}
A Pretend Market with
Buys at all Levels

Calculation with Oscillations (See Figure 3.11.)

Levels to a price of 100: 7	
Multiplier at Level 7 (see Table 2.9): 21	
Drawdown to Level 7:	
21 x $1,000	$21,000
Contracts at Level 7: 7	
Initial margin requirement:	
7 x $1,000	$7,000
Oscillations: 3	
Value of Oscillations:	
3 x $1,000	$3,000
Capital requirement	
$21,000 + $7,000 - $3,000	$25,000

Therefore, in this market we can say that, if the price falls to 100, our capital needs will be at or between $16,000 and $25,000.

B. How to Re-establish the Large Interval on the Way Down

The basic principle behind **Interval Scale Trading**^{SM} is to use a large interval during the declining market and a smaller interval in the rising market. If the market is truly falling or truly going up, there is no problem of which size interval to use. The problem of re-establishing a large interval arises during an oscillation because it is impossible to distinguish between a mere oscillation and a true change in market direction until well after the fact.

After the market begins to go up and we take a sell-buy, we have, in effect, moved our lower-most position up by one-half of a main interval. If the market continues up, the problem of deciding the direction of the market doesn't arise. We just continue to sell or sell-buy depending upon whether we own a contract at that level or not.

The problem of re-establishing a large interval does arise when the market reverses after a sell-buy and starts down. What we will do is to buy one contract one-half a main interval lower in price than our buy-sell in case we are in an uptrend oscillation. If prices continue down from there, however, we probably are in a downtrend oscillation. In that case, we don't want to buy another contract until the market has dropped at least a full main interval. (See Figure 3.12.)

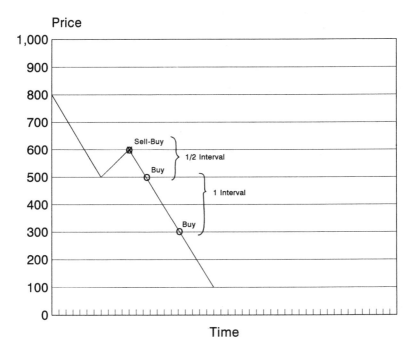

Figure 3.12
Interval Scale Trading^{SM}
Location of the Buys after the Sell-Buy

3.8. Other Features of Interval Scale Trading^{SM}

A. Short Interval Scale Trading ^{SM}

We don't use short **Interval Scale Trading**^{SM} for the same reasons we don't use short classical scale trading. (See Section 2.9.)

B. What Commodities to Trade

Any commodity suitable for classical scale trading is suitable for **Interval Scale Trading**^{SM}. (See Sections 2.7 and 2.8.)

3.9. Interval Scale Trading^{SM} a Contract

A. At What Price Do We Begin?

Interval Scale Trading^{SM} is similar to classical scale trading. The initial position is taken when the commodity penetrates into the lower one-third of a multiyear range. A fifteen year range is quite suitable for this calculation. The method for the calculation of the lower one-third of a 15-year price range is given in Sections 2.10A and B.

The only other criterion for starting **Interval Scale Trading**^{SM} is that the daily volume of the contract you choose is high enough that your order will be filled promptly and with little slippage. A daily volume of about 1,000 contracts should allow this. However, you should discuss this with your broker before actually placing the order.

B. Deciding on a Main and Intermediate Scale

Classical scale trading uses a rather small interval with the intention of capturing all the oscillation profits. The problem with a small interval is that when things go awry (which they often do), your drawdown can become overwhelming. Overwhelming drawdown can cause a debit balance and force you into liquidation.

The idea behind **Interval Scale Trading**^{SM} is to use a large interval. This is a defensive tactic. If you use a large interval and if things go awry, you don't accumulate an intolerable number of contracts. You will still have drawdown, but it will be considerably less than that of classical scale trading. To capture the oscillation profits, a sell-buy technique is used to shorten the interval as the market moves up.

How large is large? From the standpoint of potential drawdown, the larger the better. From the standpoint of potential oscillation profits, the smaller the better. Obviously, some type of compromise is necessary.

Table 3.12 contains a list of recommendations for main Intervals. This list is taken in part from The Intelligent Speculator (McGraw Hill Professional Publishing). The other values are based upon the author's experience with **Interval Scale Trading**^{SM}.

In general, five main intervals should carry you well below the lowest price of the 10-15 year range. When possible, the intermediate interval should be in the $500-$1,000 range.

Main Interval = (From Table 3.12)

Intermediate Interval = (Interval) / 2

Table 3.12
Recommend Intervals in Points

| Commodity | Recommended | |
	Main Interval	Intermediate Interval
Grains		
Wheat	24¢ ($1,200)	12¢ ($600)
Corn	18¢ ($750)	9¢ ($375)
Oats	18¢ ($750)	9¢ ($375)
Soybeans	50¢ ($2,500)	25¢ ($1,250)
Soybean Meal	$20 ($2,000)	$10 ($1,000)
Soybean Oil	200 ($1,200)	100 ($600)
Livestock and Meats		
Live Cattle	400 ($1,600)	200 ($800)
Feeder Cattle	400 ($2,000)	200 ($1,000)
Lean Hogs	400 ($1,600)	200 ($800)
Pork Bellies	700 ($2,800)	350 ($1,400)
Softs and Fibers		
Cotton	500 ($2,500)	250 ($1,250)
Cocoa	140 ($1,400)	70 ($700)
Coffee	1000 ($3,750)	500 ($1,875)
Sugar	150 ($1,680)	75 ($840)
Orange Juice	1000 ($1,500)	500 ($750)
Energies		
Crude Oil	200 ($2,000)	100 ($1,000)
Heating Oil	400 ($1,680)	200 ($840)
Unleaded Gasoline	400 ($1,680)	200 ($840)
Natural Gas	200 ($2,000)	100 ($1,000)
Metals		
Gold	$20 ($2,000)	$10 ($1,000)
Silver	20¢ ($1,000)	10¢ ($500)
Platinum	$30 $(1,500)	$15 ($750)
Copper	800 ($2,000)	400 ($1,000)

C. Ending Interval Scale Trading[SM]

Interval Scale Trading[SM] formally ends at Level 0a. Because **Interval Scale Trading**[SM] can use a sell-buy, it has a mechanism to remain in the market should you choose to do so. Instead of just selling at Level 0a, sell-buy at that level. You will remain in the market with one contract.

D. Interval Scale Trading^{SM} Rules. The Complete Game Plan

Now that we have explained how to interval trade both pretend markets, we can formalize the rules for **Interval Scale Trading**^{SM} using the sell-buy.

> 1. Establish your first position in the lower one third of a 15-year price range.
>
> 2. When the market drops after a sell-buy, buy another contract at an intermediate interval (1/2 of a main interval) below the sell-buy.
>
> 3. In all other cases, buy another contract one main interval below the last buy.
>
> 4. In a rising market, sell immediately an intermediate interval above the last buy.
>
>> A. If you don't own a contract at that level, immediately buy another contract.
>>
>> B. If you own a contract at that level, don't buy another contract.

3.10. Rollovers

Rollovers are a normal part of **Interval Scale Trading**^{SM} just as they are a normal part of classical scale trading. Expect rollovers. The procedure we will use for **Interval Scale Trading**^{SM} rollovers differs from that of classical scale trading in the following ways.

> 1. We will use an averaging technique to determine our target sell price for the rollover contract(s).
>
> 2. We will defer the rollover, if necessary, until we have some indication that the trend is up.
>
> 3. We will step out of the rollover if the market turns against us.

Accept Your Loss. If your loss is small (and only you can judge that), the best advice is to just accept the loss as part of the commodity business and continue with the new **Interval Scale Trading**^{SM}.

Rollover. If, however, you judge your losses to be too large to ignore, then you will have to roll your contract into a more distant month. This means taking new positions in a contract month whose first day notice is far in the future. For example, if you have contracts in August Soybean Meal, you would sell your August contracts and purchase December Soybean Meal.

Keep in mind that a rollover is not **Interval Scale Trading**^{SM}. We will use a different strategy in a rollover than we do in **Interval Scale Trading**^{SM}. If you want to continue **Interval Scale Trading**^{SM} the contract you are rolling over into, fine. Set up the scales, make an **Interval Scale Trading**^{SM} Table, choose your entry point, and begin a new scale trade. But don't let the new scale trade interfere with the rollover. Keep the two separate.

A. Strategy for the Rollover

<u>Don't Panic and Don't get in a Rush</u>. The market will form a bottom and it will begin an uptrend. It may take some time, but it will happen. Wait until you are "sure" an uptrend is in progress, then re-enter the market. We will discuss one technical tool to help you decide if the market has started an uptrend.

<u>Buy as Many Contracts as You Lost</u>. In our example shown below, we lost money on 3 contracts; therefore, we will buy 3 contracts in the new month.

<u>Calculate Rollover Values and Target Prices</u>. We can calculate our Rollover Values prior to the purchase of the new contracts. Once we have the purchase price for the new contracts, we can calculate our Target Sell Prices. At that point, however, we must apply some common sense.

B. When to Take the Rollover Position

There is no point in taking a rollover position if the market you are going to roll into is weak. All you would do is to add to your accumulated losses. Unfortunately, there is no sure fire way to say "The market is up!". However, there are some criteria you can use that will shift the odds more in your favor.

Your first criterion would be that the price is in the lower one half of the 15-year range, preferably in the lower one-third. This ensures (but does not guarantee) that there is some up-side potential to the market.

The second criterion would be that the daily closing price is above the 40-day moving average of the closes. This criterion means the market has shown some strength in the immediate past. There is, of course, no assurance that there will still be sufficient strength to carry the prices above your target prices. However, there has been some strength and perhaps not all of it has been used up. The signal would be a daily close above the 40-day moving average and the actual entry point would be on the next day's close, provided it also is above the 40-day moving average.

Using a 40-day moving average also provides you with a stop-loss point. Should the market close below the 40-day moving average, exit on the next day's open. Add your current losses to your accumulated losses and try again. You will get some whipsaw using this procedure; but, if you are persistent, you will **Be a Winner Trading Commodities**™.

C. Calculation of the Rollover Values

To explain the rollover calculation, we are going to assume the following about Pretend Market 2:

> After Time C (Figure 3.13), we were forced to liquidate our remaining 3 contracts at a price of 150 because first notice day was imminent. At liquidation, our losses are 3 contracts and a total of 850 points. (See Figure and Table 3.13.)

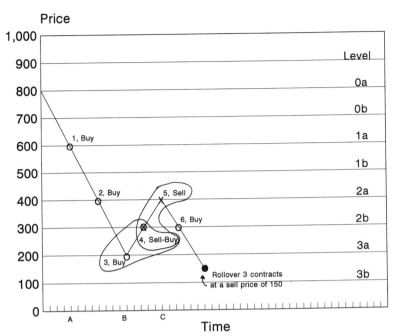

Figure 3.13
Rollover in Pretend Market 2

Table 3.13
Summary of Losses at Rollover
in Pretend Market 2
(See Figure 3.13)

Contract Purchased at Point	Purchase Price	Sell Price	Gain <loss>
1	600	150	<450>
2	400	150	<250>
6	300	150	<150>
		Total:	< 850>

Each rollover situation will be different (different number of contracts, different amount of loss, etc.). However, how we calculate the Rollover Values will be the same.

We are going to use a modified average-down strategy to determine our target prices for selling the rollover contracts. Again, using our example to explain the method, our losses were 3 contracts and 850 points. Our main interval was 200 points. Using these values, we are going to calculate three Rollover Values. The first Rollover Value would be used if we just wished to recover the losses we sustained. The second Rollover Value would be used to recover the losses and capture one-half of an interval profit per contract. The third Rollover Value would be used to recover the losses we sustained and capture a full interval profit for each contract. The calculation of these values are given in Table 3.14.

Table 3.14
Calculation of Rollover Values

Number of contracts: 3
Total Losses of the contracts: 850 points
Main Interval: 200 points

No Profit from the Rollover:

$$\text{Rollover Value 1} = \text{(Total loss)} / \text{(Number of contracts)}$$
$$= 850 / 3 = 283 \text{ points}$$

One-Half A Main Interval Profit per Contract from the Rollover:

$$\text{Rollover Value 2} = \text{Rollover Value 1} + \text{(Main Interval)} /2$$
$$= 283 + (200)/2$$
$$= 383 \text{ points}$$

Main Interval Profit per Contract from the Rollover:

$$\text{Rollover Value 3} = \text{Rollover Value 1} + \text{Main Interval}$$
$$= 283 + 200$$
$$= 483 \text{ points}$$

D. Calculation of the Target Prices

To calculate the actual Target Sell Prices we need the actual entry price. Continuing with this example, let's say we purchased three contracts at 400. The calculations of the three target prices are given in Table 3.15

Table 3.15
Calculation of Target Prices

$$
\begin{aligned}
\text{Target price 1} &= \text{Purchase price} + \text{Rollover Value 1} \\
&= 400 + 283 \\
&= 683 \\[1em]
\text{Target price 2} &= \text{Purchase price} + \text{Rollover Value 2} \\
&= 400 + 383 \\
&= 783 \\[1em]
\text{Target price 3} &= \text{Purchase price} + \text{Rollover Value 3} \\
&= 400 + 483 \\
&= 883
\end{aligned}
$$

At this point, you must use some <u>common sense</u>. Are the Target Prices reasonable? Can you expect the market to rise much above the first Target Price? Questions such as these make you focus on reasonable expectations. Should the price surpass your Target Price 1 and you want to go for Target Price 2 or 3, place a stop loss just below Target Price 1. The stop loss will allow you to recoup at least some of your loss should the market turn against you.

What do you do if the market turns against you just after you made your rollover purchases? For example, what if the market closes below the 40-day moving average? Sell the contracts! Add the new losses to the old, recalculate the Rollover Values, and be patient. Wait until you are "sure" a major bottom is in place, re-enter the market, re-calculate your target prices, and try again.

3.11. Interval Scale Trading^{SM} Without the Sell-Buy

After all is said and done, the only difference between classical scale trading and **Interval Scale Trading**^{SM} is that **Interval Scale Trading**^{SM} has up to 40% less drawdown than classical scale trading. Less drawdown means that a trader can trade the market with less capital, maintain a larger reserve in interest bearing accounts, or diversify into other commodities with less risk. Less drawdown means that the money committed in the trade is used more efficiently; that is, the percentage return is higher.

Tables 3.16 and 3.17 summarize the results of classical scale trading and **Interval Scale Trading**^{SM} of Pretend Markets 1 and 2. The final sale of the trade was taken at the same price (600 in Pretend Market 1 and 700 in Pretend Market 2) so that the results are directly comparable. Note that the drawdown is reduced by about 40% when **Interval Scale Trading**^{SM} is compared with classical scale trading. Also note that the profits are the same. This means that **Interval Scale Trading**[SM] yields the same profit but requires less capital than classical scale trading. Using **Interval Scale Trading**[SM] is a way to **Be A Winner Trading Commodities**™.

Table 3.16
Comparison Of **Interval Scale Trading**[SM] and
Classical Scale Trading
Pretend Market 1 to a Final Sale Price of 600
(See Figures 3.1 and 3.3)

	Classical Scale Trading 100 Point Interval	Interval Scale Trading[SM] 200 and 100 Point Interval
Number of Round Turn Commissions:	6	6
Capital Required at Maximum Drawdown:	$15,000	$9,000*
Total Profit:	$6,000	$6,000**
Rate of Return:	40%	67%

*Rate of Reduction = [($15,000-$9,000)/$15,000] x 100 = 40%
**If traded to a Level of 0a (a price of 700), the total profit would have been $7,000 and the rate of return, 75%.

Table 3.17
Comparison Of **Interval Scale Trading**[SM] and
Classical Scale Trading
Pretend Market 2 to a Final Sale Price of 700
(See Figures 3.8 and 3.9)

	Classical Scale Trading 100 Point Interval	Interval Scale Trading[SM] 200 and 100 Point Interval
Number of Round Turn Commissions:	8	8
Capital Required at Maximum Drawdown:	$19,000	$12,000*
Total Profit:	$8,000	$8,000**
Rate of Return:	42%	67%

*Rate of Reduction = [($19,000-$12,000)/$19,000] x 100 = 37%
**If traded to a Level of 0a (a price of 800), the total profit would have been $9,000 and the rate of return, 75%

Of special interest here is that the number of round turn commissions are the same in both systems. **Interval Scale Trading**[SM] and classical scale trading have the same commission cost in spite of the fact that **Interval Scale Trading**[SM] uses a sell-buy technique. The sell-buy does **not** increase the commission cost when compared with classical scale trading. It is identical in both methods.

However, the idea of selling and buying at the same price is totally repugnant to some individuals. Therefore, suppose we just don't do it. Let's keep everything the same, pretend we do a sell-buy, but don't actually do it. What kind of results can we expect?

What happens is:

1. The trading logic looks a little strange;
2. The commission costs are less; and
3. The end-result profit picture is not changed!

Since sell-buys are only used in an up-trending market, drawdown is not affected by their absence. Commission costs are less, as would be expected. Oscillation and trend profits are not affected. You get the same end profit whether you use a sell-buy or not! (See, for example, the comparisons of **Interval Scale Trading**[SM] with and without the sell-buy of the real markets examples in the ending chapters in this book.)

The location of the actual buys and sells appear to be without logic. Only when the trading pattern is compared with **Interval Scale Trading**[SM] using the sell-buys does it make sense. In order to make this system work, however, you have to follow the same rules (see Section 3.9D) as you would have if the sell-buy were actually being used. Buy and sell at the same prices as using the sell-buy. If you do, the profit will be the same even though some of your profit (and loss) will be deferred.

Figure 3.14 shows the **Interval Scale Trading**[SM] of Pretend Market 1 with the sell-buy and Figure 3.15 shows the same trade without the sell-buy. Recall that Pretend Market 1 has the oscillation in the up phase of the market. Table 3.18 lists the matching buys and sells for the **Interval Scale Trading**[SM] without the sell-buys. In Figure 3.15, note that no market action was taken at Points 4, 8 and 10. These were the locations of the sell-buys.

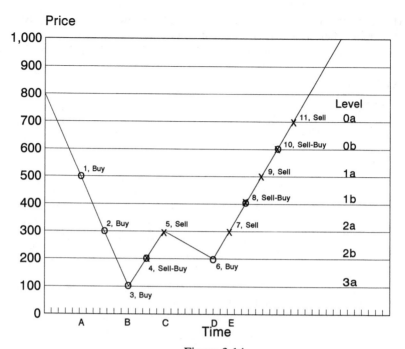

Figure 3.14
Interval Scale Trading^{SM} of
Pretend Market 1 with a Sell-Buy

Table 3.18
A Summary of All Buys and Sells
Using **Interval Scale Trading**^{SM}
In Pretend Market 1 Without the Sell-Buy
(See Figure 3.15)

Buy Point	Sell Point	Type of Profit	Profit (points)
1	11	Trend profit	200
2	9	Trend profit	200
3	5	Trend profit	200
6	7	Oscillation profit	100
		Total:	700

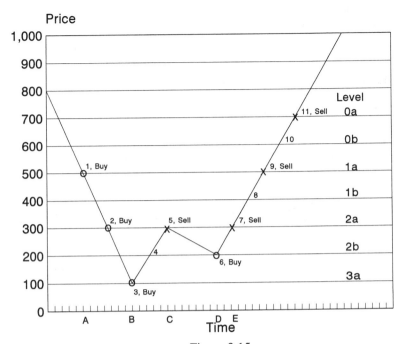

Figure 3.15
Interval Scale Trading[SM] of
Pretend Market 1 Without the Sell-Buy

Table 3.19
A Summary of All Buys and Sells
Using **Interval Scale Trading**[SM]
In Pretend Market 2 Without the Sell-Buy
(See Figure 3.17)

Buy Point	Sell Point	Type of Profit	Profit (points)
1	14	Trend profit	200
2	12	Trend profit	200
3	5	Oscillation profit	200
6	10	Trend profit	200
7	9	Trend profit	100
		Total:	900

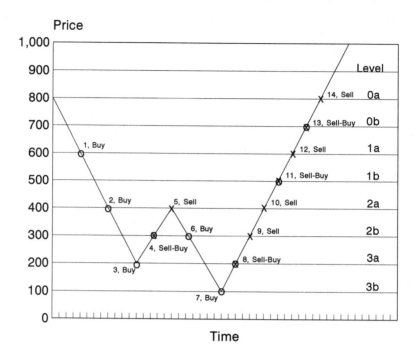

Figure 3.16
Interval Scale Trading[SM] of
Pretend market 2 with a Sell-Buy

Figures 3.16 and 3.17 and Table 3.19 provide the corresponding data for Pretend Market 2, the market with an oscillation in the down phase.

There is one disadvantage in not using the sell-buy, and that is a psychological one. Traders, such as this author, like to take profits whenever it is possible. There is kind of a jubilant feeling about taking a profit. It warms the soul. Just the reverse can be said about watching a paper profit disappear as the market drops. This author finds the loss of a paper profit depressing and discouraging. The sell-buy allows you to take profits early. This provides a psychological uplift, even though it really is an illusion.

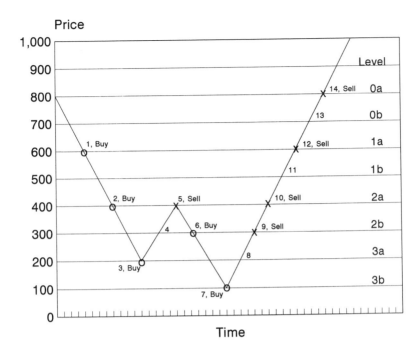

Figure 3.17
Interval Scale Trading[SM] of
Pretend Market 2 Without the Sell-Buy

Consider the pretend market shown in Figure 3.18. This is Pretend Market 2 altered so that the price at Time C is too low for a sell to take place. As the market moved from Time B to Time C, your spirits would have soared. You would have had a most rosy outlook and a paper profit of $1800. Your cheerful outlook would have changed to gloom as time went on and the price dropped. At Time D, the system required that you buy another contract, which would have been tough to do. However, without it, you would have missed the oscillation profit. By Time E you would have had a $4,000 drop in account value. A sell-buy would not have changed this end result, but you would had the satisfaction of taking $1,000 out of the market and putting it in your account. Granted, it would have been an illusory gain, but even illusions can be psychologically uplifting.

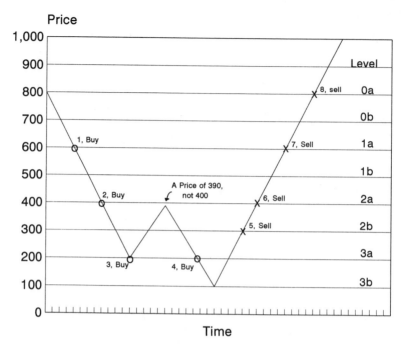

Figure 3.18
Pretend Market 2 with the Price at
Time C too Low for a Sell

In summary, you can use **Interval Scale Trading**[SM] with or without the sell-buy and obtain the same end profit. **Interval Scale Trading**[SM] with the sell-buy and classical scale trading have the same number of commissions. All three trading methods generate about the same end profit. The profit along the way, however, will vary with the method being used. **Interval Scale Trading**[SM] with the sell-buy has the same drawdown as **Interval Scale Trading**[SM] without the sell-buy. **Interval Scale Trading**[SM], regardless of whether you use the sell-buy or not, has less drawdown than classical scale trading.

Chapter 4

ParaScale Trading^{SM}

4.1. Introduction

As we have stated, there are two ways to decrease drawdown in scale trading:

1. Use a large interval; and/or
2. Take the initial position as low as possible in the down phase of the market.

We discussed using a large interval in Chapter 3, **Interval Scale Trading**^{SM} . In this chapter we will show how delaying the initial buy can be used to reduce drawdown. The scale trading method that utilizes this technique is called **ParaScale Trading**^{SM}. **ParaScale Trading**^{SM} not only reduces drawdown, but it enhances profits as well.

There are two general approaches to **ParaScale Trading**^{SM} a commodity market.

1. Enter the market with a **ParaScale Trading**^{SM} signal (the sell-buy location, see below), then after the initial purchase, revert to **Interval Scale Trading**^{SM}.

2. Enter the market using the **ParaScale Trading**^{SM} entry signal (see below), then sell one contract at each higher classical scale interval during the up phase of the market.

We will discuss each of these trading methods in the sections that follow using Pretend Markets 1 and 2. Examples of each trading method applied to real markets are given in the chapters that follow.

4.2. ParaScale Trading^{SM} Entry Followed by Interval Scale Trading^{SM}

A. The Initial Purchase. The ParaScale Trading^{SM} Entry Method

In classical scale trading and in **Interval Scale Trading**^{SM}, the initial position is taken (volume permitting) immediately after the price penetrates into the lower one third of a 15-year range. Taking the first position immediately after the market has penetrated into the lower one-third range is a "necessity" because we must have contracts in inventory before they can be sold for a profit. If the initial position is taken close to the bottom, few contracts would be purchased and profits would be scanty.

However, if fundamentals show that the commodity is being oversupplied and prices are dropping, why arbitrarily take a position in the falling market? Why not wait until the market shows some strength or that a bottom has formed. This is the idea behind **ParaScale Trading**^{SM}. Let's delay the first purchase until we have some indication that a bottom has been formed.

One key question is "How can we scale trade when we make our initial purchase near the bottom?" Let's defer an answer to this question until we have an example.

Another key question is, "How do we determine when or at what price the bottom is in place?" That is, "When do we make our initial purchase in **ParaScale Trading**^{SM}?"

There is no way to determine the price of a bottom as it is occurring. But, by definition, a bottom is a price that is a low point in the market. This means the price has to rise after it makes a bottom. Based on this obvious fact, we will use the following procedure to make our initial buy in **ParaScale Trading**^{SM}:

ParaScale Trading^{SM} Signal for Interval Scale Trading^{SM}

1. Label the levels according to the **Interval Scale Trading**^{SM} method, placing Level 1a at the one-third price of a 15-year range.

2. Delay the initial purchase until the market has:

    a. Dropped below a main level; then

    b. Buy when the market has come back one-half interval above a main level. (This is at the same price we would take our first sell-buy.)

3. Buy as many contracts as you would have had in inventory had you been **Interval Scale Trading**^{SM}.

Let's illustrate these initial purchase rules using Pretend Markets 1 and 2 (Figures 4.1 and 4.2).

1. Initial Purchase in Pretend Market 1. Oscillation in the Up Phase.

With Pretend Market 1, let's assume the one-third price is 500 and that we are using a main interval of 200 points. Therefore, Level 1a is 500 and Level 0a is 700 (see Figure 4.1). If we had been **Interval Scale Trading**^{SM} this market, we would have purchased contracts at 500, 300, and 100 (marked as 1, 2, and 3 in Figure 4.1). The bottom in Pretend Market 1 occurred at Time B (Figure 4.1). From there the price moved up to 200 (Point 4, Time C in Figure 4.1). In **Interval Scale Trading**^{SM}, we would have carried out a sell-buy at Time C because the market had moved up one-half of an interval from its last main level (a price of 100). Therefore, in **ParaScale Trading**^{SM} we make our initial purchase at 200 (Point 4, Time C, Figure 4.1).

Returning now to our question, "How can we continue scale trading when we make our first purchase near the bottom?" The answer is that we buy the number of contracts we would have held if we had been scale trading. We buy three contracts in this initial purchase because after the sell-buy in **Interval Scale Trading**^{SM} we would have owned three contracts at Point 4 (Time C in Figure 4.1).

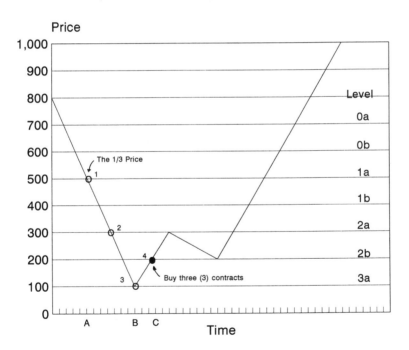

Figure 4.1
ParaScale Trading^{SM}
The Initial Buy in Pretend Market 1
(Oscillation in the Up Phase)

2. Initial Purchase in Pretend Market 2. Oscillation in the Down Phase

The same general procedure is used for Pretend Market 2. Assume the one-third price is at 600 and that we are using a 200 point main interval. Level 1a is, therefore, at 600 and Level 0a is at 800. At Point 4 (Figure 4.2) we would have made a sell-buy had we been **Interval Scale Trading**^{SM}. Therefore, our initial purchase in **ParaScale Trading**^{SM} is at Point 4 (Figure 4.2). Since we would have owned three contracts at Point 4 had we been **Interval Scale Trading**^{SM} Pretend Market 2, we buy three contracts for **ParaScale Trading**^{SM}.

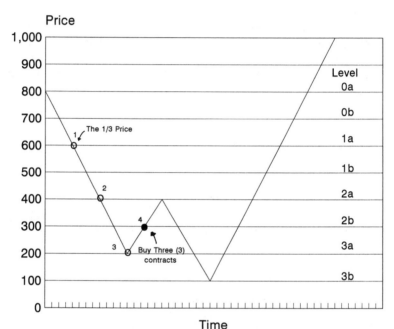

Figure 4.2
ParaScale Trading^{SM}
The Initial Buy in Pretend Market 2
(Oscillation in the Down Phase)

B. Revert to Interval Scale Trading^{SM} After the Initial Buy

The initial buy is only the first step in trading a market. After that you need a game plan to take profits from the market. After the initial buy in **ParaScale Trading**^{SM}, one approach is to continue using **Interval Scale Trading**^{SM} without the sell-buy. This approach provides a precise set of rules for buys and sells (a mechanical system).

1. Continued Trading in Pretend Market 1. Oscillation in the Up Phase

Figure 4.3 shows how **Interval Scale Trading**SM can be used to complete the trading after the initial buy.

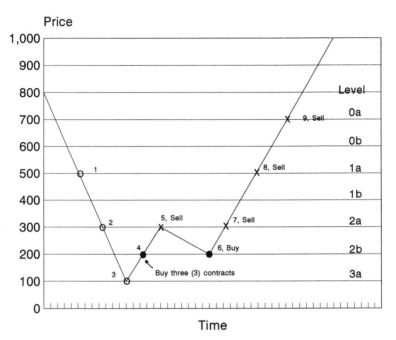

Figure 4.3
ParaScale TradingSM
Interval Scale TradingSM Pretend Market 1
After the Initial Buy
(Oscillation in the Up Phase)

<u>Drawdown.</u> There is no drawdown in **ParaScale Trading**SM Pretend Market 1 because the initial buy is after the market bottom. Our capital needs are only the initial margin for the three contracts.

```
┌─────────────────────────────────────────┐
│ Margin:                                   │
│        3 x $1,000  =    $3,000            │
│ Drawdown:                                 │
│        3 x $0  =            $0            │
│ Total Capital Needs:   $3,000            │
└─────────────────────────────────────────┘
```

Profit and Rate of Return. Table 4.1 summarizes the buys and sells. There are three trend profits and we do capture the oscillation profit by the purchase at Point 6. Our profit in **ParaScale Trading**[SM] Pretend Market 1 was 1,000 points, which is $10,000 at $10 per point, the price per point we have been using for these pretend markets.

The lowering of the purchase price of two of the three contracts in inventory dramatically enhances our profit in comparison to standard **Interval Scale Trading**[SM]. In the standard version of **Interval Scale Trading**[SM], we would have had contracts in inventory purchased at 500, 300, and 200 at Point 4 (Figure 4.3). In **ParaScale Trading**[SM] at Point 4 (Figure 4.3), all three contracts would have been purchased at 200. Because two of the contracts are purchased at a lower price but sold at the same price as we would have in **Interval Scale Trading**[SM], our profit is enhanced over that of **Interval Scale Trading**[SM]. The combination--very low capital needs ($3,000) and enhanced profit ($10,000)--results in a rate of return that is phenomenal. This is exactly what we would dearly love to have happen in the real market place.

$$\text{Rate of Return} = (\$10,000/\$3,000) \times 100 = 333\%$$

Table 4.1
ParaScale Trading[SM]
Interval Scale Trading[SM] Pretend Market 1
After the Initial Buy
(Oscillation in the Up Phase)

Buy Point	Buy Price	Sell Point	Sell Price	Profit Type	Profit (points)
4	200	9	700	trend	500*
4	200	8	500	trend	300
4	200	5	300	trend	100
6	200	7	300	oscillation	100
				Total:	1,000 points

*If the final sale were made at Level 0b, then the profit for the first contract would have been 400 points, not 500 points. The total profit would then have been 900 points, and the rate of return would have been 300%.

2. Continued Trading in Pretend Market 2. Oscillation in the Down Phase.

Similar results are observed in **ParaScale Trading**[SM] Pretend Market 2. Figure 4.4 shows the **Interval Scale Trading**[SM] without the sell-buy after the initial **ParaScale Trading**[SM] purchase. Pretend Market 2 has the oscillation in its down phase. Therefore, the bottom occurs after the **ParaScale Trading**[SM] initial purchase. As a result, **ParaScale Trading**[SM] of Pretend Market 2 does have drawdown (Point 7 in Figure 4.4). In reaching Point 7, however, we do take an oscillation profit of 100 points ($1,000).

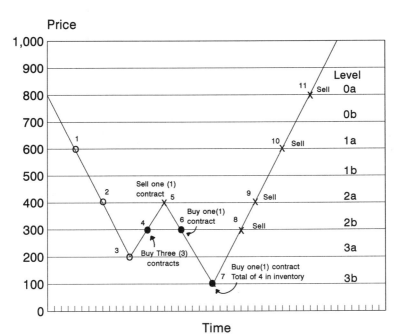

Figure 4.4
ParaScale Trading[SM]
Interval Scale Trading[SM] Pretend Market 2
After the Initial Buy

Drawdown. Our capital needs at market bottom (Point 7 in Figure 4.4) in **ParaScale Trading**[SM] Pretend Market 2 are:

121

Margin:	
4 contract times $1,000 per contract =	$4,000
Drawdown:	
3 contracts x 200 points each: 600 points	
600 points at $10 per point =	$6,000
Total: $4,000 + $6,000	$10,000
Less Oscillation Profit:	
1 oscillation profit of 100 points =	-$1,000
Total Capital needs at Point 7 (Figure 4.4):	$9,000

     Profit and Rate of Return. Table 4.2 summarizes all the buys and sells. At $10 per point, our gross profit from Pretend Market 2 was $12,000. As in the case of Pretend Market 1, the lower purchase price enhances the profits and reduces the drawdown when compared to standard **Interval Scale Trading**[SM]. The rate of return is not quite as good as that observed in Pretend Market 1 because there is drawdown. However, it is considerably better than **Interval Scale Trading**[SM] by itself.

Rate of Return than = ($12,000/$9,000) x 100 = 133%

Table 4.2
ParaScale Trading[SM]
Summary of All Buys and Sells Using
Pretend Market 2
(**Interval Scale Trading**[SM] after the Initial Buy)

Buy Point	Buy Price	Sell Point	Sell Price	Profit Type	Profit (points)
4	300	11	800	trend	500*
4	300	10	600	trend	300
4	300	5	400	oscillation	100
6	300	9	400	trend	100
7	100	8	300	trend	200
				Total:	1,200 points

*If the final sale were made at Level 0b, then the profit would have been
400 points and the total would have been 1100 points

C. Rollovers

Although not needed in the Pretend Markets shown in this chapter, in real markets it may be necessary to roll contracts over into a deferred month in order to complete the market cycle. The procedure that we will use is that described for **Interval Scale Trading**^{SM} (Section 3.10). A real market example of a **ParaScale Trading**^{SM} entry followed by **Interval Scale Trading**^{SM} is given in Chapter 10.

D. Summary of Results for the Scale Trading Family

1. Summary of Pretend Market 1

Table 4.3 summarizes the results of trading Pretend Market 1 using three members of the Scale Trading Family--classical scale trading, **Interval Scale Trading**^{SM} itself, and **ParaScale Trading**^{SM} entry followed by **Interval Scale Trading**^{SM}. As you can see, for overall results, **ParaScale Trading**^{SM} followed by **Interval Scale Trading**^{SM} is the resounding winner.

Table 4.3
Scale Trading Family
Summary of Results with Pretend Market 1

	Classical Scale Trading	Interval Scale Trading^{SM}	ParaScaleTrading^{SM} entry followed by Interval Scale Trading^{SM}
Number of round turn commissions:	6	4*	4*
Capital needed:	$15,000	$9,000	$3,000
Gross Profit:	$6,000	$6,000**	$9,000***
Rate of return:	40%	67%	300%

*If the sell-buy is used, there will be 6 round turn commissions.

**Trading was terminated at Level 0b for equal comparison of the results. If the contract had been traded to Level 0a, then the profit would have been $7,000 and the percentage return 78%.

***Trading was terminated at Level 0b for equal comparison of the results. If the contract had been traded to Level 0a, then the profit would have been $10,000 and the percentage return 333%.

2. Summary of Pretend Market 2

Table 4.4 provides a comparison of classical scale trading, **Interval Scale Trading**[SM] and **ParaScale Trading**[SM] entry followed by **Interval Scale Trading**[SM] for Pretend Market 2. Again, as you can see, for overall results, **ParaScale Trading**[SM] is the resounding winner.

Table 4.4
Summary of Scale Trading Family
Pretend Market 2

	Classical Trading	Interval Scale Trading[SM]	ParaScaleTrading[SM] entry followed by Interval Scale Trading[SM]
Number of round turn commissions:	8	5*	5*
Capital needed:	$19,000	$12,000	$9,000
Gross Profit:	$8,000	$8,000**	$11,000***
Rate of return:	42%	67%	122%

*If the sell-buy is used, there will be 8 round turn commissions.
**Trading was terminated at Level 0b for equal comparison of the results. If the contract had been traded to Level 0a, then the profit would have been $9,000 and the percentage return 75%.
***Trading was terminated at Level 0b for equal comparison of the results. If the contract had been traded to Level 0a, then the profit would have been $12,000 and the percentage return 133%.

4.3. ParaScale Trading[SM] Using a Classical Scale

ParaScale Trading[SM] followed by **Interval Scale Trading**[SM] is really just **Interval Scale Trading**[SM] with a delayed entry. The buys after the initial entry are really those of **Interval Scale Trading**[SM]. There is another way to carry out **ParaScale Trading**[SM] and that is to buy contracts only when a **ParaScale Trading**[SM] signal is given. To illustrate this technique, we will combine it with classical scale trading.

A. The Initial Entry

The central feature in **ParaScale Trading**[SM] is its delay of the first purchase in the down phase of the market--that is, we wait until we get a **ParaScale Trading**[SM] signal before entering the market. When we get the signal, we purchase the number of contracts we need to bring the inventory up to that of classical scale trading.

Therefore, to delay the first purchase -- that is to use **ParaScale Trading**[SM] -- we use the following procedure:

ParaScale Trading[SM] Signals for a Classical Scale

1. Label the levels with Level 1 set at the one-third price.

2. Delay the initial purchase until the market has:

   a. Dropped below one of the levels; and then

   b. Buy when the market has come back one-full interval above that lower level.

3. Buy the number of contracts you would have owned at that level if you had been classically scale trading.

4. Make any additional purchases only when the market has first fallen by at least two intervals and then returned by one interval.

5. Buy as many contracts as needed to bring your inventory up to that of classical scale trading.

We will illustrate Rules 1, 2 and 3 using Pretend Market 1. Rules 4 and 5, the additional entry rules, show how to use the **ParaScale Trading**[SM] signal after an oscillation in the market. We will illustrate Rule 4 and 5 with Pretend Market 2.

Real market examples of **ParaScale Trading**[SM] using a classical scale are given in the chapters that follow.

1. Initial Purchase in Pretend Market 1. Oscillation in the Up Phase

For Pretend Market 1, we will use an interval size of 100 points. We will assume the one-third price for a 15-year price range is 500. The one-third price is marked as such in Figure 4.5 (Time A). This would be the price of our initial entry if we were trading this market using classical scale trading.

The price of 500 is Level 1. Level 0 is 100 points above Level 1. The levels down from Level 1 are marked on the chart in Figure 4.5.

The lowest price in the down phase of Pretend Market 1 is 100 (Level 5; Time B; Figure 4.5). The market rises after the low and crosses Level 4 at Time C. Because the market has risen one full interval (From Level 5 to Level 4) at time C, we have a

ParaScale Trading[SM] entry signal. We buy 4 contracts at a price of 200 because we are now at Level 4.

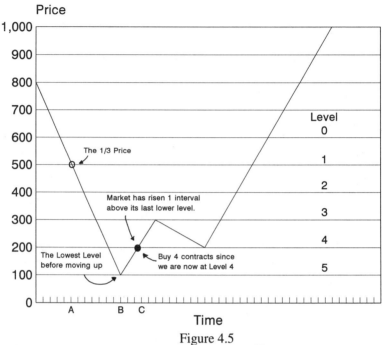

Figure 4.5
ParaScale Trading[SM]
Initial Purchase in Pretend Market 1

2. Initial Purchase in Pretend Market 2. Oscillation in the Down Phase

Pretend Market 2 has two purchases. The initial purchase is made in the same manner as that in Pretend Market 1. The market drops to a low (a price of 200, Figure 4.6) and then rises by one interval (to Level 4). This is the **ParaScale Trading**[SM] Signal. We purchase four contracts because we are at Level 4.

The second purchase is made after the oscillation and involves Rules 4 and 5. Therefore, we will discuss it in the next section (Section 4.3B2).

B. Continue Trading Using ParaScale Trading[SM]

1. Continued Trading in Pretend Market 1

Continuation of the **ParaScale Trading**[SM] of Pretend Market 1 is shown in Figure 4.7. We use a scale up technique to sell our contracts from inventory. We sell one contract at each level as the market advances. We do not use an averaging procedure as we do in rollovers. The reason is that we want to reduce our inventory as soon as we can in case the market collapses. In addition, a scale-up selling program gives us enhanced profits during the up phase of the market.

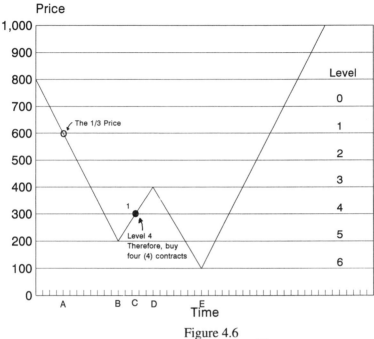

Figure 4.6
ParaScale Trading[SM]
Initial Purchase in Pretend Market 2

Pretend Market 1 does have an oscillation. It is the retracement from Level 3 to Level 4 (Time D to Time E in Figure 4.7). However, we do not buy another contract after this retracement. In classical scale trading, we would have bought another contract at Level 4 (time E), but we do not in **ParaScale Trading**[SM] because the retracement is not deep enough to trigger a new **ParaScale Trading**[SM] signal. The signal requires a retracement of at least two intervals, and in this market we only have a retracement of one interval.

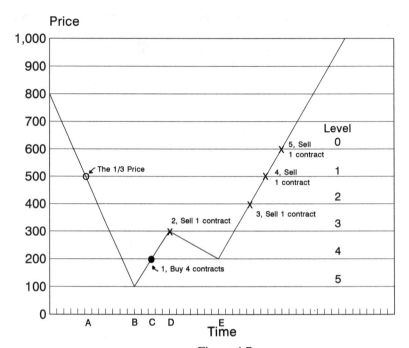

Figure 4.7
ParaScale Trading[SM]
Trading after the Initial Purchase
in Pretend Market 1

Drawdown. There is no drawdown in **ParaScale Trading**[SM] Pretend Market 1 because the initial buy occurs after the market bottom. Our capital needs are only the initial margin for the four contracts.

```
Margin:
      4 x $1,000  =   $4,000
Drawdown:
      4 x $0  =          $0
Total Capital Needs:  $4,000
```

Profit and Rate of Return. The results of trading up to Level 0 in Pretend Market 1 are summarized in Table 4.5.

128

Table 4.5
ParaScale Trading[SM]
Summary of the Buys and Sells
in Pretend Market 1

Buy Point	Buy Price	Sell Point	Sell Price	Profit Type	Profit (points)
1	200	5	600	trend	400
1	200	4	500	trend	300
1	200	3	400	trend	200
1	200	2	300	trend	100
				Total:	1000 points

At $10 per point, our profit is $10,000. The rate of return is:

$$\text{Rate of Return} = (\$10,000/\$4,000) \times 100 = 250\%$$

2. Continued Trading in Pretend Market 2

Additional **ParaScale Trading**[SM] Purchases. Pretend Market 2 has an oscillation in its down phase and, consequently, a significant retracement from that oscillation's high. The retracement consists of at least two intervals (there were actually three intervals in the retracement). The measurement for retracement is made from the oscillation high (Time D in Figure 4.8) to the new low (Time E in Figure 4.8). The measurement is not made from the last **ParaScale Trading**[SM] purchase (Time C in Figure 4.8) , unless the two happen to be the same price. This feature also allows additional purchases to be made during the up phase of a market so that oscillation profits can be captured. (Pretend Market 1 does have an oscillation in the up phase of the market, but its retracement is not two intervals deep; therefore, no **ParaScale Trading**[SM] entry signal was given.)

The signal itself is made when the market moves up after the low by at least one interval. In Pretend Market 2, this up movement was completed at Time F (Level 5 in Figure 4.8).

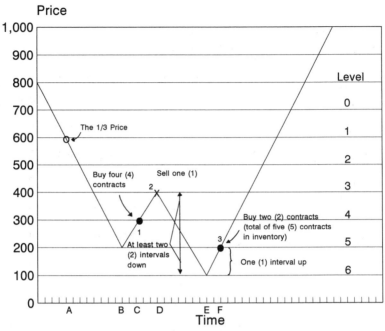

Figure 4.8
ParaScale Trading[SM]
The Additional Purchase in
Pretend Market 2

When the new signal is given, we purchase the number of contracts we would have had in inventory if we had been classically scale trading the market. At Time F in Figure 4.8, the signal was given at Level 5. Therefore, we should have five contracts in inventory. Our initial purchase was four contracts, of which we sold one at Level 3 (Time D in Figure 4.8). Therefore, prior to the new purchase we had three contracts in inventory. Thus, to bring the inventory up to a level of five we purchase two additional contracts.

Continuation of Trading. The completion of **ParaScale Trading**[SM] in Pretend Market 2 is shown in Figure 4.9.

Drawdown. Because the market dropped after the initial purchase, there is drawdown in **ParaScale Trading**[SM] of Pretend Market 2. Notice that the drawdown is not as large as that of classical scale trading (Table 4.8). The reason is that classical scale trading has made all of its purchases during the down phase, while **ParaScale Trading**[SM] makes its last purchases during the up phase. This is a general feature of **ParaScale Trading**[SM] and one of its significant advantages -- drawdown is diminished because the last purchase is made after a bottom is in place.

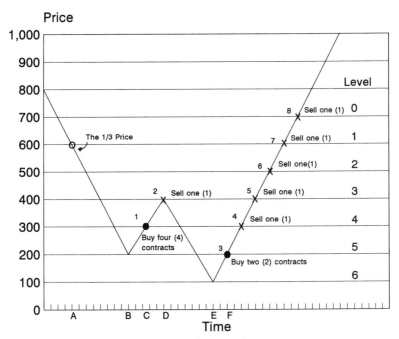

Figure 4.9
ParaScale Trading^{SM}
Pretend Market 2

Margin:		
3 contract times $1,000 per contract =		$3,000
Drawdown:		
3 contracts x 200 points each: 600 points		
600 points at $10 per point =		$6,000
Total: $3,000 + $6,000		$9,000
Less Oscillation Profit:		
1 oscillation profit of 100 points =		-$1,000
Total Capital needs at Time E (Figure 4.9)		$8,000

Profit and Rate of Return. The results of trading up to Level 0 in Pretend Market 2 are summarized in Table 4.6.

Table 4.6
ParaScale Trading[SM]
Summary of the Buys and Sells
in Pretend Market 2

Buy Point	Buy Price	Sell Point	Sell Price	Profit Type	Profit (points)
1	300	8	700	trend	400
1	300	7	600	trend	300
1	300	6	500	trend	200
1	300	2	400	oscillation	100
2	200	5	400	trend	200
2	200	4	300	trend	100
				Total:	1300 points

At $10 per point, 1300 points is equal to $13,000. Therefore the rate of return is

Rate of Return = ($13,000/$8,000) x 100 = 162%

C. Rollovers

The procedure for rollovers would be the same as described in Section 4.2C.

D. Summary of Results of the Scale Trading Family

1. Summary of Pretend Market 1

Table 4.7 summarizes the results of trading Pretend Market 1 using three members of the Scale Trading Family--classical scale trading, **Interval Scale Trading**[SM] and **ParaScale Trading**[SM] As you can see, for overall results, **ParaScale Trading**[SM] is the resounding winner.

Table 4.7
Scale Trading Family
Summary of Results with Pretend Market 1

	Classical Scale Trading	Interval Scale Trading^{SM}	ParaScale Trading^{SM}
Number of round turn commissions:	6	4*	4
Capital needed:	$15,000	$9,000	$4,000
Gross Profit:	$6,000	$6,000**	$10,000
Rate of return:	40%	67%	250%

*If the sell-buy is used, there will be 6 round turn commissions.
**Trading was terminated at Level 0b for equal comparison of the results. If the contract had been traded to Level 0a, then the profit would have been $7,000 and the percentage return 78%.

2. Summary of Pretend Market 2

Table 4.8 provides a comparison of classical scale trading, **Interval Scale Trading**^{SM} and **ParaScale Trading**^{SM} for Pretend Market 2. Again, as you can see, for overall results, **ParaScale Trading**^{SM} is the resounding winner.

Table 4.8
Summary of Scale Trading Family
Pretend Market 2

	Classical Trading	Interval Scale Trading^{SM}	ParaScale Trading^{SM}
Number of round turn commissions:	8	5*	6
Capital needed:	$19,000	$12,000	$8,000
Gross Profit:	$8,000	$8,000**	$13,000
Rate of return:	42%	67%	162%

*If the sell-buy is used, there will be 8 round turn commissions.
**Trading was terminated at Level 0b for equal comparison of the results. If the contract had been traded to Level 0a, then the profit would have been $9,000 and the percentage return 75%.

The Scale Trading Family provides a powerful mechanism to take advantage of the price movements resulting from the inherent supply and demand factors found in every freely traded commodity market. The capital requirements needed to trade these markets has now also been drastically reduced by the use of the **Interval Scale Trading**[SM] method and the **ParaScale Trading**[SM] method. Unlike typical fundamental analysis, however, once the entry point and scale have been established, the trading is entirely mechanical – providing an exact framework and the discipline required to **Be A Winner Trading Commodities**™.

In conclusion, we state:

> To **Be A Winner Trading Commodities**™, use the **ParaScale Trading**[SM] method with adequate capital.

4.4 ParaScale Trading^{SM} using Stop Orders

Reflection on the **ParaScale Trading**^{SM} technique shows that when the market has an oscillation in its down phase, drawdown will be experienced. Conversely, when there is no oscillation in the down phase, drawdown is practically non-existent. Inspection of the real market examples given in the last five chapters of this book confirms this observation. Therefore, for **ParaScale Trading**^{SM}, we can identify down phase oscillations as the major contributor to drawdown.

As we have stated several times, it is not possible to identify an oscillation from a change in the direction of the market trend. Consequently, when a **ParaScale Trading**^{SM} signal is given, we must act on it. However, we know that the danger of getting a premature signal (one that occurs during an oscillation in the market down phase) is greatest when we first begin the **ParaScale Trading**^{SM} program for a commodity contract.

With **ParaScale Trading**^{SM}, we purchase several contracts at a single price. With classical scale trading and **Interval Scale Trading**^{SM}, these purchases are spread over the down phase decline. Because, several contracts are purchased at a single price, we can use a stop loss to protect our capital and/or a trailing stop to protect profit. A similar technique would not work with classical or **Interval Scale Trading**^{SM}.

For example, we can place a stop loss just above the bottom that gave rise to the **ParaScale Trading**^{SM} signal. If the market is still in a down phase, this stop would be executed and our capital preserved. On the next **ParaScale Trading**^{SM} signal, we would re-enter the market and buy the number of contracts as dictated by the level. Other placements of a stop loss or trailing stop can be envisioned.

Using a stop loss with the **ParaScale Trading**^{SM} signal may reduce profits, but it will definitely reduce drawdown and protect capital. This allows greater diversification within the account and also allows scale trading to be used with a moderate sized account.

Chapter 5

Introduction to Real Market Examples

Pretend Markets are exactly that -- Pretend Markets. They are useful for explaining how a trading system works under rather ideal conditions and to develop trading rules. However, to see how a trading system actually works, it must be applied to real markets.

The next five chapters show real market examples of the five principal scale trading methods discussed in this book. Each chapter contains one commodity contract taken from the 1996-1998 time frame. The last of these five chapters, Chapter 10, provides rollover examples for each method (except **Interval Scale Trading**^{SM} with the sell-buy) along with their calculations.

The five scale trading methods shown are:

1. Classical scale trading;
2. **Interval Scale Trading**^{SM} with the Sell-Buy;
3. **Interval Scale Trading**^{SM} without the Sell-Buy;
4. **ParaScale Trading**^{SM} entry followed by **Interval Scale Trading**^{SM}; and
5. **ParaScale Trading**^{SM}.

The real market examples were not chosen to provide back testing of the scale trading systems. Rather they were chosen to provide real market examples showing the principles of scale trading. Each market is traded under as identical conditions as possible so that the five trading methods and their results can be directly compared.

The first three commodity examples were chosen to illustrate successful scale trading. The fourth example was chosen to illustrate a contract in which scale trading fails, and the fifth to illustrate rollovers.

The following rules were used for these trades:

1. The market had to move through a price for execution.

For example, a sell did not occur in the classical scale trading of August 1996 Feeder Cattle at 60.00 because the price of 60 was only touched.

2. On a buy, if the market opened below the desired purchase price, the open price, rather than the desired price was used.

3. On a sell, if the market opened above the desired price, the open price, rather than the desired price was used.

4. There was no trading over the top of the scale.

5. When the scale was complete, the price had to drop below the starting price before a new position was taken.

For example, see Pork Bellies July 1998.

6. Commissions and potential slippage were ignored.

The last seven months of the contract's life were used for presentations. Volume toward the start of the contract's life was ignored. If the first day's prices of the contract were below the starting price, the close on the first day was used for entry. The last day shown in the presentations was the day before the month of termination. (For example, July 31 for an August contract.)

For consistent comparisons of the trading methods, trades were taken whenever a signal was given. For example, in real time trading many of the trades taken toward the end of the contracts' life would have been taken in a deferred month rather than as shown. Also, for ease of chart study, starting prices are not the exact calculated one-third prices, but rather one-third prices rounded to a convenient number.

Chapter 6

August 1996 Feeder Cattle

This contract was chosen to illustrate the enormous advantage of using a delayed entry (**ParaScale Trading**^{SM}) for scale trading. August 1996 Feeder Cattle collapsed in April of 1996, made a V-bottom, and then recovered in a spectacular fashion. Both scale trading methods that used the **ParaScale Trading**^{SM} initial entry method had little or no drawdown while those that did not use this entry method have very large drawdowns.

The starting price for this commodity contract was the one-third value rounded to a price of 64. The contract was traded for seven months starting on 1/2/96 and ending on 7/31/96. The prices on 1/2/96 were below 64; therefore, according to the rules of classical and **Interval Scale Trading**^{SM}, the initial purchase was made on the first day of the contract shown in Figures 6.1, 6.2 and 6.3.

All trading methods showed a profit and reasonable rate of return. However, the drawdown, and thus the rate of return, varied dramatically from method to method. (See the summary table at the end of this chapter.).

A contract of Feeder Cattle is 50,000 lbs with a minimum fluctuation of 0.025 cents per lb (2½ points; $12.50). The data in this chapter is rounded to two decimal places and, where appropriate, expressed in points (1 point = $5.00). Thus a 200 point interval would equate to $1,000. The initial margin of a contract of Feeder Cattle is about $900.

6.1. Classical Scale Trading

A. Trading Results

The buys and sells for the classical scale trading of this market are shown in Figure 6.1 and are summarized in Table 6.1.

In March of 1996, the price touched 60 but did not move through this value. Therefore, according to the assumptions stated in Chapter 5, no signal was given.

At $5.00 per point, the gross profit was:

Gross profit ($5.00 per point x 1,850 points) = $9,250

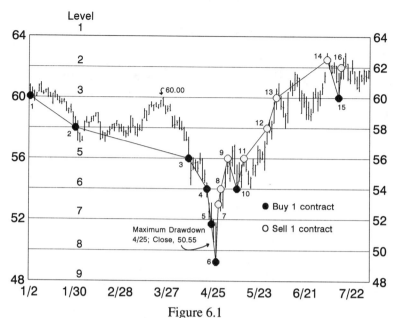

Figure 6.1
Classical Scale Trading
August 1996 Feeder Cattle
(Interval, 200 points; Starting Price, 64.00)

Table 6.1
Summary of Buys and Sells for
August 1996 Feeder Cattle
(See Figure 6.1)

Buy			Sell			Profit <Loss>
Figure Point	Date	Price	Figure Point	Date	Price	(Points)
1	1/02	60.05	14	7/05	62.50	245
2	1/30	58.00	13	6/04	60.00	200
3	4/10	56.00	12	5/29	58.00	200
4	4/22	54.00	9	5/03	56.00	200
5	4/24	51.70	8	4/30	54.00	230
6	4/26	49.25	7	4/29	53.53	375
10	5/09	54.00	11	5/14	56.00	200
15	7/12	60.00	16	7/15	62.00	200
					Total:	1,850

140

B. Drawdown and Capital Needs

The maximum drawdown occurred on 4/25 at a closing price of 50.55. The maximum drawdown actually occurred before the purchase of the last contract in the down phase of the market. This unusual event occurred because the market closed up (at 51.50) after the purchase of Contract 6, which would have occurred during the day. Therefore, at the close of 4/26 the drawdown was less than it was on 4/25 even though another contract had been purchased. The drawdown calculation for the five contracts to a price of 50.55 is shown in Table 6.2.

Table 6.2
Classical Scale Trading
Drawdown for August 1996
Feeder Cattle
(See Figure 6.1)

Buy			Close on	Drawdown
Figure Point	Date	Price	4/25	(Points)
1	1/02	60.05	50.55	950
2	1/30	58.00	50.55	745
3	4/10	56.10	50.55	555
4	4/22	54.00	50.55	345
5	4/24	51.70	50.55	115
			Total:	2,710

At $5.00 per point, the drawdown for the trading was:

Drawdown ($5.00 per point x 2,710 points) = $13,550

Capital needs include margin. The initial margin requirements for Feeder Cattle is about $900. Therefore, at maximum drawdown, the capital requirements would have been:

Margin (5 contracts x $900 per contract): $4,500
Drawdown: $13,500

Total Capital needs: $18,500

C. Rate of Return for Classical Scale Trading of August 1996 Feeder Cattle

Classical scale trading yielded a gross profit of $9,250. Eight round turn commissions were required. The total capital needed for the trade was $18,500. Therefore, the rate of return for the classical scale trading of this contract (excluding commissions) was:

$$\text{Rate of return} = (\$9{,}250/\$18{,}500) \times 100 = 50\%$$

6.2 Interval Scale Trading^{SM} with the Sell-Buy

A. Trading Results

The buys and sells for **Interval Scale Trading^{SM}** this contract using the sell-buy technique are shown in Figure 6.2 and are summarized in Table 6.3. Note that the three sell-buys (Points 4, 8, and 10 in Figure 6.2) are listed in both the buy and sell columns.

In the next three chapters, we will provide charts and tables for both techniques so that readers can verify for themselves that the overall results of these two techniques are identical except for the greater number of round turn commissions required when using the sell-buy technique. We will, however, discontinue any further discussion of **Interval Scale Trading^{SM}** with the sell-buy.

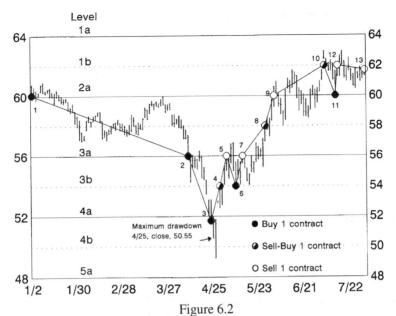

Figure 6.2
Interval Scale Trading[SM] Using the Sell-Buy
August 1996 Feeder Cattle
(Main Interval, 400 points; Intermediate Interval, 200 points;
Starting price, 64)

Table 6.3
Interval Scale Trading[SM] Using the Sell-Buy
Summary of Buys and Sells for
August 1996 Feeder Cattle
(See Figure 6.2)

Buy			Sell			Profit <Loss>
Figure Point	Date	Price	Figure Point	Date	Price	(Points)
1	1/02	60.05	10	7/05	62.50	245
2	4/10	56.00	8	5/29	58.00	200
3	4/24	51.70	4	4/30	54.00	230
4	4/30	54.00	5	5/03	56.00	200
6	5/09	54.00	7	5/14	56.00	200
8	5/29	58.00	9	6/04	60.00	200
10	7/05	62.50	13	7/31	61.77	<73>
11	7/12	60.00	12	7/15	62.00	200
					Total:	1,402

B. Drawdown and Capital Needs

The drawdown calculations for **Interval Scale Trading**[SM] using the sell-buy are shown in Table 6.4. For discussion and calculations, see Section 6.3B.

Table 6.4
Interval Scale Trading[SM] using the Sell-Buy
Drawdown for August 1996 Feeder Cattle
(See Figure 6.2)

Buy			Close on	Drawdown
Figure Point	Date	Price	4/25	(Points)
1	1/02	60.05	50.55	950
2	4/10	56.00	50.55	545
3	4/24	51.70	50.55	115
			Total:	1,610

Table 6.5
Interval Scale Trading[SM] Without the Sell-Buy
Summary of Buys and Sells for August 1996
Feeder Cattle
(See Figure 6.2)

Buy			Sell			Profit <Loss>
Figure Point	Date	Price	Figure Point	Date	Price	(Points)
1	1/02	60.05	10	7/31	61.77	172
2	4/10	56.00	7	6/04	60.00	400
3	4/24	51.70	4	5/03	56.00	430
5	5/09	54.00	6	5/14	56.00	200
8	7/12	60.00	9	7/15	62.00	200
					Total:	1,402

6.3. Interval Scale Trading^{SM} without the Sell-Buy

A. Trading Results

The buys and sells for **Interval Scale Trading**^{SM} without the sell-buy technique are shown in Figure 6.3 and are summarized in Table 6.5

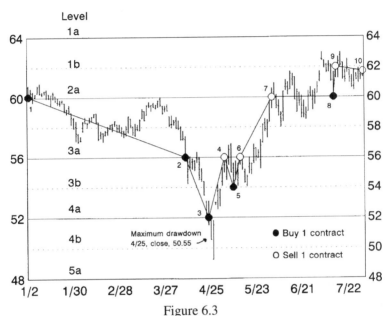

Figure 6.3
Interval Scale Trading^{SM} Without the Sell-Buy
August 1996 Feeder Cattle
(Main Interval, 400 points; Intermediate Interval, 200 points;
Starting price, 64)

Although some of the buys and sells are located at slightly different prices, the overall results of **Interval Scale Trading**^{SM} with and without the sell-buy are identical.

The gross profit for the contract was:

Gross profit ($5.00 per point x 1,402 points) = $7,010

B. Drawdown and Capital Needs

The drawdown results for **Interval Scale Trading**^{SM} without the sell-buy are summarized in Table 6.6.

Table 6.6
Interval Scale Trading^{SM} without the Sell-Buy
Drawdown for August 1996 Feeder Cattle
(See Figure 6.3)

Figure Point	Buy		Close on	Drawdown
	Date	Price	4/25	(Points)
1	1/02	60.05	50.55	950
2	4/10	56.00	50.55	545
3	4/24	51.70	50.55	115
			Total:	1,610

Only three contracts were purchased during the drawdown phase of the market compared to the six contracts purchased using classical scale trading. Consequently, there was drawdown:

Drawdown ($5.00 per point x 1,610 points) = $8,050

As stated before, the margin for Feeder Cattle is about $900. Therefore, the total capital needs were:

Margin (3 contracts x $900 per contract): $2,700
Drawdown: $8,050

Total Capital needs: $10,750

In comparison to classical scale trading, the reduction in total capital needs was about 42%:

$$\frac{(\$18,500 - \$10,750)}{\$18,500} \times 100 = 42\%$$

This is about the best reduction of capital needs that can be achieved using **Interval Scale Trading**^{SM}. When there are oscillations in the down phase of the market, the percentage reduction is considerably less. (For example, see August 1998 Soybean Meal, Chapter 9).

C. Rate of Return for Interval Scale Trading^{SM} without the Sell-Buy of August 1996 Feeder Cattle

The gross profit from **Interval Scale Trading**^{SM} was $7,010. Five round turn commissions were needed. The capital needed was $10,750. Therefore, the rate of return for **Interval Scale Trading**^{SM} was:

$$\text{Rate of Return} = (\$7,010/\$10,750) \times 100 = 65\%$$

6.4. ParaScale Trading^{SM} Entry Followed by Interval Scale Trading^{SM}

A. Trading Results

The buys and sells for **ParaScale Trading**^{SM} entry followed by **Interval Scale Trading**^{SM} are given in Figure 6.4 and summarized in Table 6.7.

Using this scale trading technique, the initial purchase is made when you would normally make the first sell-buy in **Interval Scale Trading**^{SM} using the sell-buy. (Compare Figure 6.4, Point 1, with Figure 6.2, Point 4.) Three contracts were purchased at Point 1 because this is the number of contracts you would have had in inventory had you been **Interval Scale Trading**^{SM} the contract using the sell-buy.

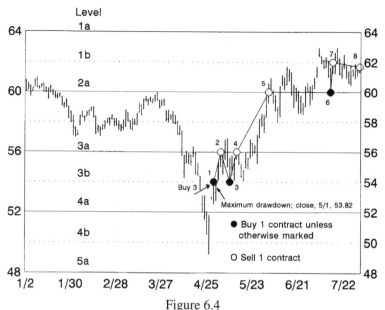

Figure 6.4
ParaScale Trading^{SM} Followed by **Interval Scale Trading**^{SM}
August 1996 Feeder Cattle
(Main Interval, 400 points; Intermediate Interval, 200 points;
Starting price, 64)

Table 6.7
ParaScale Trading^{SM} Followed by **Interval Scale Trading**^{SM}
Summary of Buys and Sells for August 1996 Feeder Cattle
(See Figure 6.4)

Buy			Sell			Profit <Loss>
Figure Point	Date	Price	Figure Point	Date	Price	(Points)
1	4/30	54.00	8	7/31	61.77	777
1	4/30	54.00	5	6/04	60.00	600
1	4/30	54.00	2	5/03	56.00	200
3	5/09	54.00	4	5/14	56.00	200
6	7/12	60.00	7	7/15	62.00	200
					Total:	1,977

From Point 1 (Figure 6.4) to the end of the contract's life, **Interval Scale Trading**^{SM} without the sell-buy was followed. (Compare Figures 6.3 and 6.4.)

The gross profit obtained using this trading technique was:

Gross profit ($5.00 per point x 1,977 points) = $9,885

This profit is greater than that obtained using either classical scale trading ($9,250) or **Interval Scale Trading**^{SM} by itself ($7,010).

B. Drawdown and Capital Needs

The really impressive feature of this trading technique is the very small drawdown that was experienced (54 points, $270). This small drawdown was possible because the initial purchase delay placed the first purchase just after the contract's lowest bottom. A very small drawdown using this scale trading method will always be the case if the down phase of the market has no oscillations and the bottom is made with a V pattern. This, unfortunately, cannot be predicted before the fact.

The drawdown calculations are given in Table 6.8.

Table 6.8
ParaScale Trading^{SM} Followed by **Interval Scale Trading**^{SM}
Drawdown for August 1996 Feeder Cattle
(See Figure 6.4)

Buy			Close on	Drawdown
Figure Point	Date	Price	5/1	(Points)
1	4/30	54.00	53.82	18
1	4/30	54.00	53.82	18
1	4/30	54.00	53.82	18
			Total:	54

The total capital requirements for this trading method for this contract are:

Margin (3 contracts x $900 per contract): $2,700
Drawdown ($5.00 per points x 54 points): $270

Total Capital needs: $2,970

In comparison to classical scale trading, this scale trading technique reduced the capital needs by about 84%.

$$\frac{(\$18,500 - \$2,970)}{\$18,500} \times 100 = 84\%$$

This reduction in capital needs is superior to that which can be achieved by **Interval Scale Trading**[SM] alone. This improved reduction is due to a combination of the larger interval used by **Interval Scale Trading**[SM] and the delayed entry accomplished by **ParaScale Trading**[SM].

C. Rate of Return for ParaScale Trading[SM] followed by Interval Scale Trading[SM] with the Sell-Buy of August 1996 Feeder Cattle

The gross profit was $9,885. Five round turn commissions were required. Drawdown was $2,970. Therefore, the rate of return (excluding commissions) was:

$$\text{Rate of return} = (\$9,885/\$2,970) \times 100 = 333\%$$

The combination of higher gross profit and lower capital needs for this trade dramatically enhances the rate of return in comparison to classical scale trading and **Interval Scale Trading**[SM]

6.5. ParaScale Trading[SM]

A. Trading Results

Even more dramatic results were obtained using **ParaScale Trading**[SM] combined with a classical scale. The buys and sells are shown in Figure 6.5 and the results summarized in Table 6.9.

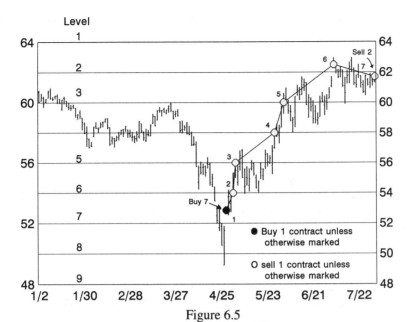

Figure 6.5
ParaScale Trading[SM]
August 1996 Feeder Cattle
(Interval, 200 points; Starting price, 64)

Table 6.9
ParaScale Trading[SM]
Summary of Buys and Sells for August 1996 Feeder Cattle
(See Figure 6.5)

Buy			Sell			Profit <Loss>
Figure Point	Date	Price	Figure Point	Date	Price	(Points)
1	4/29	53.00	7	7/31	61.77	877
1	4/29	53.00	7	7/31	61.77	877
1	4/29	53.00	6	7/05	62.50	950
1	4/29	53.00	5	6/14	60.50	750
1	4/29	53.00	4	5/29	58.00	500
1	4/29	53.00	3	5/03	56.00	300
1	4/29	53.00	2	5/02	54.40	140
					Total:	4,394

All seven contracts were purchased on the first signal then sold using a scale-up technique -- each sell being one interval (200 points) higher than the previous one. The gross profit with the seven contracts was:

151

Gross profit ($5.00 per point x 4,394 points) = $21,970

While profits of this type can be expected with **ParaScale Trading**[SM], it takes a disciplined trader to go long seven contracts in a market of this type at the time the signal was given. Huge **ParaScale Trading**[SM] profits with no drawdown can only be realized if the market has no oscillations in its down phase, makes a final V bottom, and then has a substantial up move. As we have said, it is not possible to predict these events before the fact. Had this market only been making an oscillation in its down phase, there would have been drawdown.

B. Drawdown and Capital Needs

There was no drawdown in this market. All contracts would have been purchased during the day and the market closed at the entry price of 53.00. Even if the buy order was not filled until the next day, the results would have been substantially the same. (The price range for the next day was 54.20-52.55.)

The total capital needs for **ParaScale Trading**[SM] of this contract were:

Margin (7 contracts x $900 per contract):	$6,300
Drawdown:	$0

Total Capital needs:	$6,300

The capital requirements are greater than that of **ParaScale Trading**[SM] followed by **Interval Scale Trading**[SM] because more contracts were purchased.

In comparison to classical scale trading the reduction in required capital was:

$$\frac{(\$18,500 - \$6,300)}{\$18,500} \times 100 = 65\%$$

C. Rate of Return for ParaScale Trading^SM August 1996 Feeder Cattle

The gross profit was $21,970. A total of seven round turn commissions were required. The capital needs were $6,300. Therefore, the rate of return (excluding commissions) was :

$$\text{Rate of Return} = (\$21,970/\$6300) \times 100 = 348\%$$

6.6. Summary of Scale Trading Results for August 1996 Feeder Cattle

Table 6.10 provides a summary of the trading results for August 1996 Feeder Cattle using the scale trading family discussed in this chapter. The entry for **Interval Scale Trading**^SM in Table 6.10 refers to both **Interval Scale Trading**^SM with and without the sell-buy since their results are identical.

Table 6.10
Summary of Trading Results
for August 1996 Feeder Cattle

	Classical Scale Trading	Interval Scale Trading^SM	ParaScale Trading^SM then Interval Scale Trading^SM	ParaScale Trading^SM
Gross Profit:	$9,250	$7,010	$9,885	$21,970
Number of Round Turn Commissions	8	5*	5	7
Capital Needs:				
Margin:	$4,500	$2,700	$2,700	$6,300
Drawdown:	$13,500	$8,050	$270	0
Total:	$18,500	$10,750	$2,970	$6,300
Reduction of Capital Needs:	--	42%	84%	65%
Rate of Return	50%	65%	333%	348%

*Eight round-turn commissions would have been required if the sell-buy was used.

153

Chapter 7

December 1996 High Grade Copper

December 1996 High Grade Copper was chosen as an example to illustrate the effect of a long, sideways market movement. The contract had a fast decline to its bottom on 6/25 followed by a very slow recovery. The market did terminate with an up trend; therefore, all scale trading family members showed a profit.

The one-third price for this contract was rounded to a starting price of 100. Seven months of the contract were traded. The starting date was 5/1/96 and the ending date 11/27/96.

A contract of High Grade Copper is 25,000 lbs with prices quoted in cents per lb. A minimum fluctuation is 0.05 cents per pound (5 points; $12.50). The data in this chapter, where appropriate, are expressed in points (1 point = $2.50). Thus, a 400 point scale equates to $1,000. The initial margin requirement is about $1,600 per contract.

7.1. Classical Scale Trading

A. Trading Results

The buys and sells are shown in Figure 7.1 and are summarized in Table 7.1.

At $2.50 per point, the gross profit was:

Gross profit ($2.50 per point x 3,700 points) = $9,250

B. Drawdown and Capital Needs

The drawdown for classical scale trading is summarized in Table 7.2. The contract's lowest close was on 6/25.

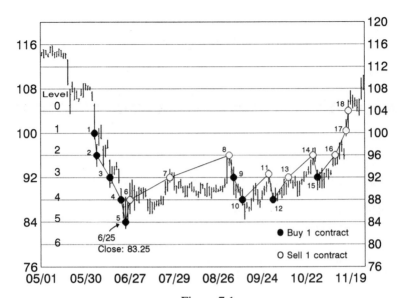

Figure 7.1
Classical Scale Trading
December 1996 High Grade Copper
(Interval, 400 points; Starting Price, 100.00)

Table 7.1
Summary of Buys and Sells for
December 1996 High Grade Copper
(See Figure 7.1)

Buy			Sell			Profit <Loss>
Figure Point	Date	Price	Figure Point	Date	Price	(Points)
1	06/05	100.00	18	11/18	104.00	400
2	06/06	96.00	17	11/15	100.40	440
3	06/14	92.00	8	09/03	96.00	400
4	06/21	88.00	7	07/25	92.00	400
5	06/25	84.00	6	06/27	88.00	400
9	09/05	92.00	14	10/25	96.00	400
10	09/11	88.00	11	09/27	92.60	460
12	10/01	88.00	13	10/10	92.00	400
15	10/29	92.00	16	11/08	96.00	400
					Total:	3,700

Table 7.2
Classical Scale Trading
Drawdown for
December 1996 High Grade Copper
(See Figure 7.1)

	Buy		Close on	Drawdown
Figure Point	Date	Price	6/25	(Points)
1	6/05	100.00	83.25	1675
2	6/06	96.00	83.25	1275
3	6/14	92.00	83.25	875
4	6/21	88.00	83.25	475
5	6/25	84.00	83.25	75
			Total:	4,375

At $2.50 per point, the drawdown for the trading was:

Drawdown ($2.50 per point x 4,375 points) = $10,937

Capital needs include margin. The initial margin requirements for High Grade Copper is about $1,600. Therefore, at maximum drawdown, the capital requirements would have been:

Margin (5 contracts x $1,600 per contract): $8,000
Drawdown: $10,937

Total Capital needs: $18,937

C. Rate of Return for Classical Scale Trading of December 1996 High Grade Copper

Classical scale trading yielded a gross profit of $9,250. Nine round-turn commissions were required. The total capital needs for the trade were $18,937. Therefore, the rate of return for the classical scale trading of this Copper contract (excluding commissions) was:

Rate of return = ($9,250/$18,937) x 100 = 49%

157

7.2. Interval Scale Trading[SM] with the Sell-Buy

The end results for **Interval Scale Trading**[SM] with and without the sell-buy technique are identical. Therefore, this section contains the figure showing the buys and sells for **Interval Scale Trading**[SM] using the sell-buy technique (Figure 7.2) and tables that summarize the trading and drawdown (Tables 7.3 and 7.4). General discussion of **Interval Scale Trading**[SM] and the calculations are deferred until Section 7.3.

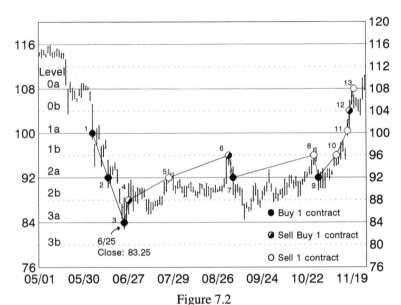

Figure 7.2
Interval Scale Trading[SM] Using the Sell-Buy
December 1996 High Grade Copper
(Main Interval, 800 points; Intermediate Interval, 400 points;
Starting price, 100.00)

Table 7.3
Interval Scale Trading^{SM} Using the Sell-Buy
Summary of Buys and Sells for December 1996
High Grade Copper
(See Figure 7.2)

Buy			Sell			Profit <Loss>
Figure Point	Date	Price	Figure Point	Date	Price	(Points)
1	06/05	100.00	12	11/18	104.00	400
2	06/14	92.00	6	09/03	96.00	400
3	06/25	84.00	4	06/27	88.00	400
4	06/27	88.00	5	07/25	92.00	400
6	09/03	96.00	11	11/15	100.40	440
7	09/05	92.00	8	10/25	96.00	400
9	10/29	92.00	10	11/08	96.00	400
12	11/18	104.00	13	11/26	108.00	400
					Total:	3,240

Table 7.4
Interval Scale Trading^{SM} using the Sell-Buy
Drawdown for December 1996 High Grade Copper
(See Figure 7.2)

Buy			Close on	Drawdown
Figure Point	Date	Price	6/25	(Points)
1	6/04	100.00	83.25	1,675
2	6/14	92.00	83.25	875
3	6/28	84.00	83.25	75
			Total:	2,625

7.3. Interval Scale Trading^{SM} without the Sell-Buy

A. Trading Results

The buys and sells for **Interval Scale Trading**^{SM} without the sell-buy technique are shown in Figure 7.3 and are summarized in Table 7.5

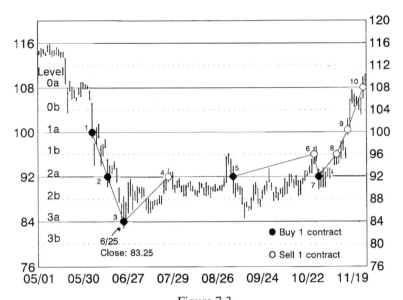

Figure 7.3
Interval Scale Trading[SM] Without the Sell-Buy
December 1996 High Grade Copper
(Main Interval, 800 points; Intermediate Interval, 400 points;
Starting price, 100.00)

Table 7.5
Interval Scale Trading[SM] Without the Sell-Buy
Summary of Buys and Sells for December 1996
High Grade Copper
(See Figure 7.3)

Buy			Sell			Profit <Loss>
Figure Point	Date	Price	Figure Point	Date	Price	(Points)
1	06/04	100.00	10	11/26	108.00	800
2	06/14	92.00	9	11/15	100.40	840
3	06/25	84.00	4	07/25	92.00	800
5	09/05	92.00	6	10/25	96.00	400
7	10/29	92.00	8	11/08	96.00	400
					Total:	3,240

The gross profit for the contract was:

Gross profit ($2.50 per point x 3,240 points) = $8,100

160

The overall results of **Interval Scale Trading**[SM] with and without the sell-buy are identical, even though some of the buys and sells are located at slightly different prices,

B. Drawdown and Capital Needs

The drawdown results for **Interval Scale Trading**[SM] without the sell-buy are summarized in Table 7.6. Both **Interval Scale Trading**[SM] techniques have the same number of contracts in inventory at maximum drawdown. Therefore, the capital needs of both techniques are identical.

Table 7.6
Interval Scale Trading[SM] without the Sell-Buy
Drawdown for December 1996 High Grade Copper
(See Figure 7.3)

Buy			Close on	Drawdown
Figure Point	Date	Price	6/25	(Points)
1	6/04	100.00	83.25	1,675
2	6/14	92.00	83.25	875
3	6/28	84.00	83.25	75
			Total:	2,625

Only three contracts were purchased during the drawdown phase of the market compared to the five contracts purchased using classical scale trading. Consequently, drawdown was less. The drawdown was:

Drawdown ($2.50 per point x 2,625 points) = $6,562

As stated previously, the margin for High Grade Copper is about $1,600. Therefore the total capital needs were:

Margin (3 contracts x $1,600 per contract):	$4,800
Drawdown:	$6,562

Total Capital needs:	$11,362

The reduction in total capital needs was about 40% when compared with classical scale trading.

$$\frac{\$18{,}937 - \$11{,}362)}{\$18{,}937} = x \ 100 \ = \ 40\%$$

C. Rate of Return for Interval Scale Trading^{SM} of December 1996 High Grade Copper

The gross profit from **Interval Scale Trading**^{SM} the December 1996 High Grade Copper contract was $8,100. Five round-turn commissions were required. The total capital needs were $11,362. Therefore, the rate of return (excluding commissions) was:

$$\text{Rate of Return} \ = \ (\$8{,}100/\$11{,}362) \ x \ 100 \ = \ 71\%$$

7.4. ParaScale Trading^{SM} Entry followed by Interval Scale Trading^{SM}

A. Trading Results

The buys and sells for **ParaScale Trading**^{SM} entry followed by **Interval Scale Trading**^{SM} are given in Figure 7.4 and summarized in Table 7.7.

With this scale trading technique, the initial purchase is made when you normally would make the first sell-buy in **Interval Scale Trading**^{SM} using the sell-buy technique. (Compare Figure 7.2, Point 4, with Figure 7.4, Point 1.) In this Copper contract, three contracts were purchased at Point 1 (Figure 7.4) because this is the number of contracts you would have had in inventory had you been **Interval Scale Trading**^{SM} the contract using the sell-buy.

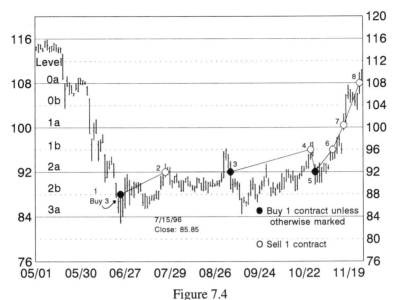

Figure 7.4
ParaScale Trading[SM] Followed by **Interval Scale Trading**[SM]
December 1996 High Grade Copper
(Main Interval, 800 points; Intermediate Interval, 400 points;
Starting price, 100.00)

Table 7.7
ParaScale Trading[SM] Followed by **Interval Scale Trading**[SM]
Summary of Buys and Sells for December 1996 High Grade Copper
(See Figure 7.4)

Buy			Sell			Profit <Loss>
Figure Point	Date	Price	Figure Point	Date	Price	(Points)
1	06/25	88.00	8	11/26	108.00	2,000
1	06/25	88.00	7	11/15	100.40	1,240
1	06/25	88.00	2	07/25	92.00	400
3	09/05	92.00	4	10/25	96.00	400
5	10/29	92.00	6	11/08	96.00	400
					Total:	4,440

163

From Point 1 (Figure 7.4) to the end of the contract's life, **Interval Scale Trading**^{SM} without the sell-buy is followed. (Compare Figures 7.3 and 7.4.)

The gross profit obtained using this trading technique was:

Gross profit ($2.50 per point x 4,440 points) = $11,100

B. Drawdown and Capital Needs

The initial purchase of three contracts occurs after the contract low. However, just after the purchase, the market declined below that initial purchase price. It closed at 85.85 on 7/15. Therefore, drawdown was experienced.

The drawdown is summarized in Table 7.8.

Table 7.8
ParaScale Trading^{SM} Followed by **Interval Scale Trading**^{SM}
Drawdown for December 1996 High Grade Copper
(See Figure 7.4)

Buy			Close on	Drawdown
Figure Point	Date	Price	7/15	(Points)
1	6/25	88.00	85.85	215
1	6/25	88.00	85.85	215
1	6/25	88.00	85.85	215
			Total:	645

Drawdown ($2.50 per contract x 645 points) = $1,612

As in the case of August 1996 Feeder Cattle (Section 6.4), the drawdown experienced in this contract using this scale trading was rather nominal. This small drawdown was possible because there were no oscillations in the down phase of the market.

The total capital requirements for this trading method for this Copper contract are:

Margin (3 contracts x $1,600 per contract):	$4,800
Drawdown:	$1,612

Total Capital needs:	$6,412

In comparison with classical scale trading, the capital needs have been reduced by about 66% by using the **ParaScale Trading**^{SM} entry method followed by **Interval Scale Trading**^{SM}.

$$\frac{(\$18,937 - \$6,412)}{\$18,927} \times 100 = 66\%$$

As was observed in the August 1996 Feeder Cattle example, this is a far better reduction than can be achieved by **Interval Scale Trading**^{SM} alone. As before, this improved reduction is due to a combination of the larger interval used with **Interval Scale Trading**^{SM} and the delayed entry accomplished by **ParaScale Trading**^{SM}.

D. Rate of Return for ParaScale Trading^{SM} Entry followed by Interval Scale Trading^{SM} of December 1996 High Grade Copper

The combination of higher gross profit and lower capital needs for this trade dramatically enhances the rate of return in comparison with classical scale trading and **Interval Scale Trading**^{SM}. The gross profit for this trading technique was $11,100. Five round turn commissions were required. The capital needs were $6,412. Therefore, the rate of return (excluding commissions) was:

Rate of return = ($11,100/$6,412) x 100 = 173%

7.5. ParaScale Trading

A. Trading Results

Equally dramatic results were obtained using **ParaScale Trading**[SM] in combination with a classical scale. The buys and sells are shown in Figure 7.5 and the results are summarized in Table 7.9.

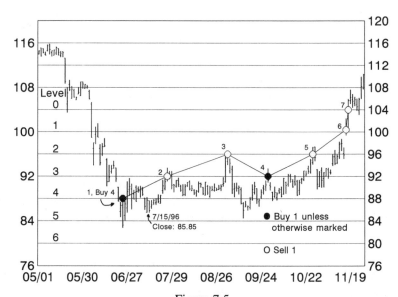

Figure 7.5
ParaScale Trading[SM]
December 1996 High Grade Copper
(Interval, 400 points; Starting price, 100.00)

There were two **ParaScale Trading**[SM] signals given in this contract. The first (Point 1, Figure 7.5) was the initial purchase.

Prior to the initial purchase at Point 1, there appears to be other **ParaScale Trading**[SM] signals. However, none of them truly qualify for the initial signal. For this contract, the starting price was 100. Therefore, the price had to dip below 100 before the start of a signal could even be considered. This qualification eliminated the price action at

166

Table 7.9
ParaScale Trading[SM]
Summary of Buys and Sells for December 1996
High Grade Copper
(See Figure 7.5)

Buy			Sell			Profit <Loss>
Figure Point	Date	Price	Figure Point	Date	Price	(Points)
1	6/27	88.00	7	11/18	104.00	1,600
1	6/27	88.00	6	11/15	100.40	1,240
1	6/27	88.00	3	09/03	96.00	800
1	6/27	88.00	2	07/25	92.00	400
4	9/27	92.60	5	10/25	96.00	340
					Total:	4,380

Gross profit ($2.50 x 4,380) = $10,950

the start of the chart (5/1 to 5/30). Just after the prices dropped below 100, there was a price rise of one interval. However, this did not qualify as a signal because it had not been preceded by a drop of two or more intervals after the prices penetrated the starting price of 100.

The initial signal--(a) penetration of starting price, (b) a price drop of two or more intervals, (c) followed by a price rise of one interval--occurred at Point 1 in Figure 7.5. Since at Point 1 we were at Level 4, we purchased four contracts.

The second **ParaScale Trading**[SM] signal occurred after Point 3 in Figure 7.5. The price range on 9/3 (Point 3) was 96.20 - 94.10. Therefore, Level 2 (96.00) had been breached. The market then dropped two (almost three) levels before moving up. The move from Level 4 to Level 3 qualifies Point 4 (Figure 7.5) as a **ParaScale Trading**[SM] signal--a move down of at least two levels followed by a one level up move. Had the decline from Level 3 continued to just beyond Level 5 (a three level down move), then the signal would have been given when the market moved above 88.00, the Level 4 price.

Only one contract was purchased at Point 4 because the market is at Level 3 (thus requiring three contracts in inventory). The initial purchase was four contracts and two of those were sold (Points 2 and 3). Therefore, there were two contracts left in inventory prior to the purchase of the one contract at Point 4.

B. Drawdown and Capital Needs

The drawdown is summarized in Table 7.10.

Table 7.10
ParaScale Trading[SM]
Drawdown for December 1996
High Grade Copper
(Figure 7.5)

Figure Point	Buy		Close on 7/15	Drawdown (Points)
	Date	Price		
1	6/27	88.00	85.85	215
1	6/27	88.00	85.85	215
1	6/27	88.00	85.85	215
1	6/27	88.00	85.85	215
			Total:	860

Drawdown ($2.50 per point x 860 points) = $2,150

The initial purchase (Point 1, Figure 7.5) occurred after the contract low. However, there was a dip in prices on 7/15 after the initial purchase. Therefore, the trade did have drawdown (860 points). The amount of drawdown is greater than **ParaScale Trading**[SM] followed by **Interval Scale Trading**[SM] because more contracts were purchased.

The total capital needs for **ParaScale Trading**[SM] this contract were:

Margin (4 contracts x $1,600 per contract):	$6,400
Drawdown:	$2,150

Total Capital needs:	$8,550

In comparison with classical scale trading, the reduction in required capital was:

$$\frac{(\$18{,}937 \, - \, \$8{,}550)}{\$18{,}937} \text{ x } 100 \; = \; 54\%$$

C. Rate of Return for ParaScale Trading^{SM} of December 1996 High Grade Copper

The gross profit was $10,950. A total of five round-turn commissions were required. The capital needs were $8,550. Therefore, the rate of return (excluding commissions) was:

$$\text{Rate of Return} = (\$10,950/\$8,550) \times 100 = 128\%$$

7.6. Summary of Scale Trading Results for December 1996 High Grade Copper

Table 7.11 provides a summary of the trading results for December 1996 High Grade Copper for the scale trading family discussed in this chapter. The **Interval Scale Trading^{SM}** included Table 7.11 refers to both **Interval Scale Trading^{SM}** with and without the sell-buy since their results are identical.

Table 7.11
Summary of Trading Results
for December 1996 High Grade Copper

	Classical Scale Trading	Interval Scale Trading^{SM}	ParaScale Trading^{SM} then Interval Scale Trading^{SM}	ParaScale Trading^{SM}
Gross Profit:	$9,250	$8,100	$11,100	$10,950
Number of Round Turn Commissions	9	5	5	5
Capital Needs:				
Margin:	$8,000	$4,800	$4,800	$6,400
Drawdown:	$10,937	$6,562	$1,612	$2,150
Total:	$18,937	$11,362	$6,412	$8,550
Reduction of Capital Needs:	--	40%	66%	54%
Rate of Return	49%	71%	173%	128%

169

Chapter 8

July 1998 Pork Bellies

July 1998 Pork Bellies was selected as an example of a commodity contract that has an oscillation in the down phase of its market that occurred below the one-third price level. July 1998 Pork Bellies recovered after its down phase and rallied enough that all members of the scale trading family showed a profit.

In real time trading, the contracts taken as trades toward the end of the July 1998 Pork Bellies contract would probably have been taken in a deferred contract month. They are included in this contract month for consistent trading so that a direct comparison of the different scale trading methods can be made.

The one-third price for this contract was rounded to a starting price of 55.00. Seven months of the contract were traded. The starting date was 12/1/97 and the ending date was 6/30/98.

A contract of Pork Bellies is 40,000 lbs with a minimum fluctuation of 0.025 cents per lb (2½ points; $10). The data in this chapter is rounded to two decimal places and, where appropriate, expressed in points (1 point = $4.00). The initial margin for a contract of Pork Bellies is about $1,600.

8.1. Classical Scale Trading

A. Trading Results

The buys and sells for the classical scale trading of this commodity contract are shown in Figure 8.1 and summarized in Table 8.1.

At $4.00 per point, the gross profit was:

Gross profit ($4.00 per point x 4,065 points) = $16,260

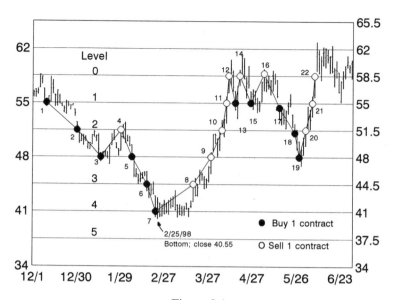

Figure 8.1
Classical Scale Trading
July 1998 Pork Bellies
(Interval, 350 points; Starting Price, 55)

Table 8.1
Classical Scale Trading
Summary of Buys and Sells for July 1998 Pork Bellies
(See Figure 8.1)

Buy			Sell			Profit <Loss>
Figure Point	Date	Price	Figure Point	Date	Price	(Points)
1	12/09	55.00	12	04/09	58.50	350
2	12/30	51.50	11	04/08	55.00	350
3	01/15	48.00	4	01/29	51.50	350
5	02/05	48.00	10	04/06	52.40	440
6	02/17	44.50	9	03/30	48.00	350
7	02/23	41.00	8	03/18	44.50	350
13	04/15	55.00	14	04/17	58.50	350
15	04/24	55.00	16	05/04	58.80	380
17	05/13	54.40	22	06/05	58.50	410
18	05/22	51.15	21	06/04	55.00	385
19	05/27	48.00	20	06/01	51.50	350
					Total:	4,065

B. Drawdown and Capital Needs

The maximum drawdown occurred on 2/25, after Point 7 (Figure 8.1). During the down phase, there was one oscillation profit, Point 3 to Point 4. The profit from this oscillation is subtracted from the overall drawdown. (In Table 8.2, this profit is shown in < > to indicate it is to be subtracted from the total drawdown.)

Table 8.2
Classical Scale Trading
Drawdown for
July 1998 Pork Bellies
(See Figure 8.1)

Figure Point	Buy		Close on 2/25	Drawdown (Points)
	Date	Price		
1	12/09	55.00	40.55	1,445
2	12/30	51.50	40.55	1,095
5	02/05	48.00	40.55	745
6	02/17	44.50	40.55	395
7	02/23	41.00	40.55	45
Less Oscillation profit				
3	01/15	48.00	51.50	<350>
			Total:	3,375

At $4.00 per point, the drawdown for the trading was:

Drawdown ($4.00 per point x 3,375 points) = $13,500

At total of five contracts were held at the time of maximum drawdown. The margin requirement for a contract of Pork Bellies is about $1,600 per contract. Therefore, the total capital needs at maximum drawdown were:

Margin (5 contracts at $1,600 per contract):	$8,000
Drawdown:	$13,500

Total Capital Needs:	$21,500

C. Rate of Return for Classical Scale Trading of July 1998 Pork Bellies

Classical scale trading of this contract yielded a gross profit of $16,260. A total of 11 round-turn commissions were required. The total capital needs for the trade were

$21,500. Therefore, the rate of return for the classical scale trading of this contract (excluding commissions) was:

$$\text{Rate of return } (\$16,260/\$21,500) \times 100 = 75\%$$

8.2. Interval Scale Trading^{SM} with the Sell-Buy

A. Trading Results

The final results for **Interval Scale Trading**^{SM} with and without the sell-buy technique are identical. Therefore, this section contains the figure showing the buys and sells for **Interval Scale Trading**^{SM} using the sell-buy technique (Figure 8.2) and the tables that summarize the trading and drawdown (Tables 8.3 and 8.4). A general discussion of **Interval Scale Trading**^{SM} and the calculations are deferred until Section 8.3.

Table 8.3
Interval Scale Trading^{SM} with the Sell-Buy
Summary of Buys and Sells for July 1998 Pork Bellies
(See Figure 8.2)

Buy			Sell			Profit <Loss>
Figure Point	Date	Price	Figure Point	Date	Price	(Points)
1	12/09	55.00	10	04/09	58.50	350
2	01/15	48.00	3	01/29	51.50	350
3	01/29	51.50	9	04/08	55.00	350
4	02/05	48.00	8	04/06	52.40	440
5	02/23	41.00	6	03/18	44.80	380
6	03/18	44.80	7	03/30	48.00	320
10	04/09	58.50	20	06/08	62.00	350
11	04/15	55.00	12	04/17	58.50	350
13	04/24	55.00	14	05/04	58.80	380
15	05/13	54.40	19	06/05	58.50	410
16	05/27	48.00	17	06/01	51.50	350
17	06/01	51.50	18	06/04	55.00	350
					Total:	4,380

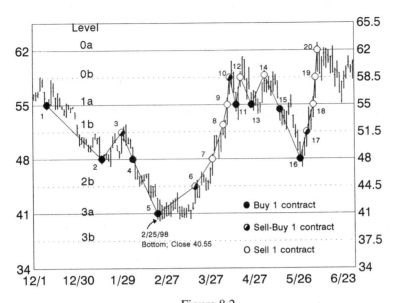

Figure 8.2
Interval Scale Trading[SM] with the Sell-Buy
July 1998 Pork Bellies
(Main Interval, 700 points; Intermediate Level, 350 points;
Starting Price, 55)

Table 8.4
Interval Scale Trading[SM] with the Sell-Buy
Drawdown for
July 1998 Pork Bellies
(See Figure 8.2)

Buy			Close on	Drawdown
Figure Point	Date	Price	2/25	(Points)
1	12/09	55.00	40.55	1,445
3	01/29	51.50	40.55	1,095
4	02/05	48.00	40.55	745
5	02/23	41.00	40.55	45
Less Oscillation profit				
2	01/15	48.00	51.50	<350>
			Total:	2,980

175

8.3. Interval Scale Trading^{SM} without the Sell-Buy

A. Trading Results

The buys and sells for **Interval Scale Trading**^{SM} without the sell-buy are shown in Figure 8.3 and summarized in Table 8.5.

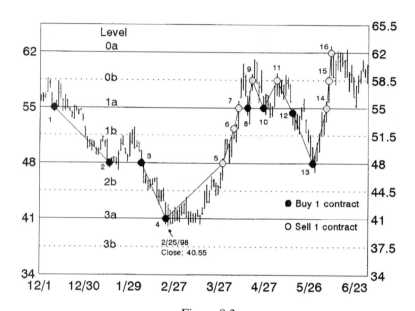

Figure 8.3
Interval Scale Trading^{SM} without the Sell-Buy
July 1998 Pork Bellies
(Main Interval, 700 points; Intermediate Level, 350 points; Starting Price, 55)

At $4.00 per point, the gross profit was:

$$\text{Gross profit (\$4.00 per point x } 4{,}380) = \$17{,}520$$

Comparison of Figure 8.1 with Figures 8.2 and 8.3 show **Interval Scale Trading**^{SM} did not miss any of the oscillation profits that classical scale trading captured. The gross profit for classical scale trading was 4,065 points ($16,260) while that for **Interval Scale Trading**^{SM} was 4,380 points ($17,520). The difference, 315 points, is due to the higher top of the scale in **Interval Scale Trading**^{SM}. The top of the scale in classical scale trading is 58.50 while that of **Interval Scale Trading**^{SM} is 62.00 (Level 0a). Therefore, in this market, classical scale trading scaled out before **Interval Scale Trading**^{SM}.

Table 8.5
Interval Scale Trading^{SM} without the Sell-Buy
Summary of Buys and Sells for
July 1998 Pork Bellies
(See Figure 8.3)

Buy			Sell			Profit <Loss>
Figure Point	Date	Price	Figure Point	Date	Price	(Points)
1	12/09	55.00	16	06/08	62.00	700
2	01/15	48.00	7	04/08	55.00	700
3	02/05	48.00	6	04/06	52.40	440
4	02/23	41.00	5	03/30	48.00	700
8	04/15	55.00	9	04/17	58.50	350
10	04/24	55.00	11	05/04	58.80	380
12	05/13	54.40	15	06/05	58.50	410
13	05/27	48.00	14	06/04	55.00	700
					Total:	4,380

B. Drawdown and Capital Needs

The drawdown for **Interval Scale Trading**^{SM} of this Pork Bellies contract is summarized in Table 8.6.

Table 8.6
Interval Scale Trading^{SM} without the Sell-Buy
Drawdown for
July 1998 Pork Bellies
(See Figure 8.3)

Buy			Close on	Drawdown
Figure Point	Date	Price	2/25	(Points)
1	12/09	55.00	40.55	1,445
3	01/15	48.00	40.55	745
3	02/05	48.00	40.55	745
4	02/23	41.00	40.55	45
			Total:	2,980

At $4.00 per point, the maximum drawdown for the contract was:

177

Drawdown ($4.00 per point x 2,980 points) = $11,920

A total of four contracts were held at the time of maximum drawdown. The margin requirement for a contract of Pork Bellies is about $1,600 per contract. Therefore, the total capital needs at maximum drawdown were:

Margin (4 contracts at $1,600 per contract):	$6,400
Drawdown:	$11,920

Total Capital Needs:	$18,320

Interval Scale Trading[SM] with the sell-buy had an oscillation profit in the down phase of the market (Point 2 to Point 3 in Figure 8.2). **Interval Scale Trading**[SM] without the sell-buy did not have an oscillation profit at this point. In spite of this difference, both trading methods had identical amounts of drawdown, contracts in inventory, and capital needs at the time of maximum drawdown. The reason for this identicalness is the relative placement of the buys. The profit gained by using the sell-buy was lost during the decline from Point 3 to Point 4 (Figure 8.2).

The net effect of an oscillation in the down phase of a market upon **Interval Scale Trading**[SM] is to increase drawdown. This occurs because at least one additional contract is purchased for each oscillation in the down-phase. If there are enough oscillations in the down phase, the drawdown for **Interval Scale Trading**[SM] will equal (but not exceed) that of classical scale trading.

The reduction in drawdown in comparison with classical scale trading for this contract is only 16%. Markets with no oscillations in their down phase show reductions in the 40 to 42% range (See Chapters 6 and 7).

$$\frac{(\$21,500 - \$18,320)}{\$21,500} = 15\%$$

C. Rate of Return for Interval Scale Trading[SM] of July 1998 Pork Bellies

The gross profit from **Interval Scale Trading**[SM] was $17,520. A total of eight round-turn commissions were required. The total capital needs at maximum drawdown were $18,320. Therefore, the rate of return (excluding commissions) was:

Rate of return = ($17,520/$18,320) x 100 = 95%

8.4. ParaScale Trading^{SM} Entry followed by Interval Scale Trading^{SM}

A. Trading Results

The buys and sells for **ParaScale Trading**^{SM} entry followed by **Interval Scale Trading**^{SM} are given in Figure 8.4 and summarized in Table 8.7.

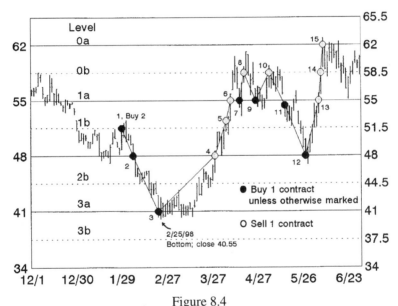

Figure 8.4
ParaScale Trading^{SM} followed by **Interval Scale Trading**^{SM}
July 1998 Pork Bellies
(Main Interval, 700 points; Intermediate Level, 350 points;
Starting Price, 55)

Table 8.7
ParaScale Trading^{SM} followed by **Interval Scale Trading**^{SM}
Summary of Buys and Sells for
July 1998 Pork Bellies
(See Figure 8.4)

Buy			Sell			Profit <Loss>
Figure Point	Date	Price	Figure Point	Date	Price	(Points)
1	01/29	51.50	15	06/08	62.00	1,050
1	01/29	51.50	6	04/08	55.00	350
2	02/05	48.00	5	04/06	52.40	440
3	02/23	41.00	4	03/30	48.00	700
7	04/15	55.00	8	04/17	58.50	380
9	04/24	55.00	10	05/04	58.80	350
11	05/13	54.40	14	06/05	58.50	410
12	05/27	48.00	13	06/04	55.00	700
					Total:	4,380

At $4.00 per point, the gross profit was:

$$\text{Gross profit ($4.00 per point x 4,380)} = \$17,520$$

In this market, there was no advantage gained by using the **ParaScale Trading**^{SM} entry method. The signal was given at the first sell-buy (Point 1, Figure 8.4; see also Figure 8.2, Point 3). Since this signal occurred during the down phase oscillation, the potential advantage was lost. The market declined below the entry price and the trading system reverted to **Interval Scale Trading**^{SM} without the sell-buy. The end result is that the two trading systems are identical.

B. Drawdown and Capital Needs

The drawdown for the **ParaScale Trading**^{SM} entry followed by **Interval Scale Trading**^{SM} is summarized in Table 8.8.

Table 8.8
ParaScale Trading[SM] followed by **Interval Scale Trading**[SM]
Drawdown for
July 1998 Pork Bellies
(See Figure 8.4)

Buy			Close on	Drawdown
Figure Point	Date	Price	2/25	(Points)
1	01/29	51.50	40.55	1,095
1	01/29	51.50	40.55	1,095
2	02/05	48.00	40.55	745
3	02/23	41.00	40.55	45
			Total:	2,980

At \$4.00 per point, the maximum drawdown for the contract was:

Drawdown (\$4.00 per points x 2,980 points) = \$11,920

Comparison of Table 8.8 with Table 8.6 will show that the drawdown for the two methods are identical.

At total of four contracts were held at the time of maximum drawdown. The margin requirement for a contract of Pork Bellies is about \$1,600 per contract. Therefore, the total capital needs at maximum drawdown were:

Margin (4 contract at \$1,600 per contract):	\$6,400
Drawdown:	\$11,920

Total Capital Needs:	\$18,320

Again, this requirement is identical to that of **Interval Scale Trading**[SM].

C. Rate of Return for ParaScale Trading[SM] Entry followed by Interval Scale Trading[SM]

The gross profit obtained from using the **ParaScale Trading**[SM] entry followed by **Interval Scale Trading**[SM] was \$17,520. A total of eight round-turn commissions were required. The total capital needs at maximum drawdown were $18,320. Therefore, the rate of return (excluding commissions) was:

$$\text{Rate of return} = (\$17,520/\$18,320) \times 100 = 95\%$$

This result, like the other results in this Section, is identical to that observed for **Interval Scale Trading**[SM] alone.

8.5. ParaScale Trading[SM]

A. Trading Results

The buys and sells for **ParaScale Trading**[SM] are given in Figure 8.5 and summarized in Table 8.9.

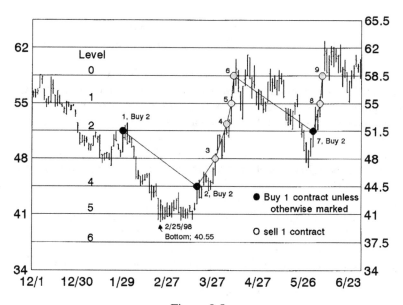

Figure 8.5
ParaScale Trading[SM]
July 1998 Pork Bellies
(Level, 350 points; Starting Price, 55)

Table 8.9
ParaScale Trading[SM]
Summary of Buys and Sells for
July 1998 Pork Bellies
(See Figure 8.5)

Buy			Sell			Profit <Loss>
Figure Point	Date	Price	Figure Point	Date	Price	(Points)
1	01/29	51.50	6	04/09	58.50	700
1	01/29	51.50	5	04/08	55.00	350
2	03/18	44.50	4	04/06	52.40	790
2	03/18	44.50	3	03/30	48.00	350
7	06/01	51.50	9	06/05	58.50	700
7	06/01	51.50	8	06/04	55.00	350
					Total:	3,240

At $4.00 per point, the gross profit was:

$$\text{Gross profit ($4.00 per point x 3,240)} = \$12,960$$

The gross profit for **ParaScale Trading**[SM] was the smallest of the scale trading family for this commodity contract. This was due in part to the fact that a purchase was not made on the market low as was done with the other members of the scale trading family. (For example, see Figure 8.1, Point 7 and compare this with Figure 8.5). The smaller gross profit was also due in part to the fact that the potential oscillation profits during the March to April time frame were missed. (See Figure 8.5 after Point 6 and compare that time period with that of classical scale trading , Figure 8.1 after Point 12.)

However, the smaller gross profit is offset by the fact that **ParaScale Trading**[SM] also had the smallest drawdown, the highest reduction of capital needs, and the highest rate of return of the scale trading family. In effect, a smaller gross profit was exchanged for a more efficient use of capital.

B. Drawdown and Capital Needs

The drawdown for the **ParaScale Trading**[SM] is summarized in Table 8.10

Table 8.10
ParaScale Trading[SM]
Drawdown for
July 1998 Pork Bellies
(See Figure 8.5)

Buy			Close on	Drawdown
Figure Point	Date	Price	2/25	(Points)
1	1/29	51.50	40.55	1,095
1	1/29	51.50	40.55	1,095
			Total:	2,190

At $4.00 per point, the maximum drawdown for the contract was:

Drawdown ($4.00 per points x 2,190 points) = $8,760

A total of two contracts were held at the time of maximum drawdown. The margin requirement for a contract of Pork Bellies is about $1,600 per contract. Therefore, the total capital needs at maximum drawdown were:

Margin (2 contracts at $1,600 per contract): $3,200
Drawdown: $8,760

Total Capital Needs: $11,960

One of the general characteristics of **ParaScale Trading**[SM] is that the final purchases are made after the market's bottom is in place. This is clearly illustrated by two of the buys in this contract. The purchase at Point 2 (Figure 8.5) came after the contract's major bottom was in place. The second illustration is the buy at Point 7 (Figure 8.5), where the purchase was made after the bottom of a major retracement. This characteristic is one of the major contributors to the lower drawdown using the **ParaScale Trading**[SM] method.

The reduction in drawdown in comparison with classical scale trading for this contract is 44%. Markets with no oscillations in their down phase show higher reductions. (See Chapters 6 and 7).

$$\frac{(\$21,500 - \$11,960)}{\$21,500} = 44\%$$

C. Rate of Return for ParaScale Trading^{SM} of July 1998 Pork Bellies

ParaScale Trading^{SM} of this contract yielded a gross profit of $12,960 . A total of 6 round-turn commissions were required. The total capital needs are $11,960. Therefore, the rate of return (excluding commissions) was:

Rate of return = ($12,960/$11,960) x 100 = 108%

8.6. Summary of Scale Trading Results for July 1998 Pork Bellies

Table 8.11 provides a summary of the trading results for July 1998 Pork Bellies for the scale trading family discussed in this chapter. The **Interval Scale Trading**^{SM} included in Table 8.11 refers to both **Interval Scale Trading**^{SM} with and without the sell-buy since their results are identical.

Table 8.11
Summary of Trading Results for
July 1998 Pork Bellies

	Classical Scale Trading	Interval Scale Trading^{SM}	ParaScale Trading^{SM} then Interval Scale Trading^{SM}	ParaScale Trading^{SM}
Gross Profit:	$16,260	$17,520	$17,520	$12,960
Number of Round-Turn Commissions	11	8	8	6
Capital Needs:				
Margin:	$8,000	$6,400	$6,400	$3,200
Drawdown:	$13,500	$11,920	$11,920	$8,700
Total:	$21,500	$18,320	$18,320	$11,960
Reduction of Capital Needs:	--	16%	16%	44%
Rate of Return	75%	95%	95%	108%

Chapter 9

August 1998 Soybean Meal

August 1998 Soybean Meal was selected as an example to illustrate that when the commodity contract does not end in an up move, all members of the scale trading family lose money. When this happens, a rollover will be required. (An example of a rollover is presented in Chapter 10). In this chapter, we will only look at the relative drawdowns and losses of the scale trading family.

August 1998 Soybean Meal had a significant decline, reaching the bottom of the contract in June of 1998. A sharp market reaction against the downtrend appeared to signal that the final bottom was in place. Instead, the market faded, and after a few minor oscillations, collapsed at its end.

Technically, the major oscillation in this market would be considered to be in the up phase of the market because the bottom on 6/10/98 was not violated. However, market action in deferred contracts after this contract terminated has shown the oscillation is actually in the market's down phase.

As in the Pork Bellies example (Chapter 8), in real time trading some of the trades taken towards the end of this contract would have been taken in a deferred contract month. But, they are included in this contract month for consistent trading so that a direct comparison of the different scale trading methods can be made.

The one-third price for this contract was rounded to a starting price of 185. Seven months of the contract were traded. The starting date was 1/2/98 and the ending date was 7/31/98.

A contract of Soybean Meal is 100 tons with price quotations in dollars per ton. The minimum fluctuation is $0.10 per ton (1 point; $10). The data in this chapter is expressed in points where appropriate (1 point = $10.00). The initial margin for a contract of Soybean Meal is about $950.

9.1. Classical Scale Trading

A. Trading Results

The buys and sells for the classical trading of this commodity contract are shown in Figure 9.1 and summarized in Table 9.1.

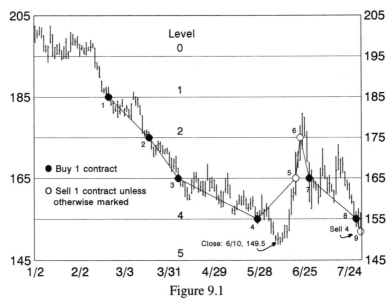

Figure 9.1
Classical Scale Trading
August 1998 Soybean Meal
(Interval, 100 points; Starting Price, 185)

Table 9.1
Classical Scale Trading
Summary of Buys and Sells for
August 1998 Soybean Meal
(See Figure 9.1)

Buy			Sell			Profit <Loss>
Figure Point	Date	Price	Figure Point	Date	Price	(Points)
1	2/20	185.0	9	7/31	151.9	<331>
2	3/18	175.0	9	7/31	151.9	<231>
3	4/06	165.0	6	6/23	175.0	100
4	5/27	155.0	5	6/19	165.0	100
7	6/29	165.0	9	7/31	151.9	<131>
8	7/29	155.0	9	7/31	151.9	<31>
					Total:	<524>

Two oscillation profits were taken before the market collapsed at the end of the contract's life. However, the market retracement erased these profits and, by the end of the trading, a loss of 524 points had accumulated. At $10.00 per point, the loss was:

Gross loss ($10.00 per point x 524 points) = <$5,240>

B. Drawdown and Capital Needs

For classical scale trading, the maximum drawdown occurred on 6/10/98 at a close of 149.5 (after Point 4, Figure 9.1). Four contracts were in inventory at this time. The oscillations occurred after Point 4, and therefore, did not decrease the drawdown.

Table 9.2
Classical Scale Trading
Drawdown for
August 1998 Soybean Meal
(See Figure 9.1)

	Buy		Close on	Drawdown
Figure Point	Date	Price	6/10	(Points)
1	2/20	185	149.5	355
2	3/18	175	149.5	255
3	4/06	165	149.5	155
4	5/27	155	149.5	55
			Total:	820

At $10 per point the drawdown was:

Drawdown ($10.00 per point x 820 points) = $8,200

The initial margin for Soybean Meal is about $950 per contracts. Four contracts were in inventory at maximum drawdown. Therefore, the capital needs would have been:

Margin (4 contracts x $950 per contract): $3,800
Drawdown: $8,200

Total: $12,000

C. Rate of Return for August 1998 Soybean Meal

Classical scale trading had a net loss of <$5,240>. A total of six round-turn commissions were required. The total capital needs were $12,000. Therefore the rate of return (excluding commissions) was:

$$\text{Rate of return} = (<\$5,240>/\$12,000) \times 100 = <43\%>$$

This means that almost one-half of the capital needed to trade the market was lost as a true loss (not a paper loss) at the end of the trade.

9.2. Interval Scale Trading^{SM} with the Sell-Buy

A. Trading Results

The final results for **Interval Scale Trading^{SM}** with and without the sell-buy technique are identical. Therefore, this section contains the figure showing the buys and sells for **Interval Scale Trading^{SM}** using the sell-buy technique (Figure 9.2) and tables that summarize the trading and drawdown (Tables 9.3 and 9.4). A general discussion of **Interval Scale Trading^{SM}** and the calculations are deferred until Section 9.3

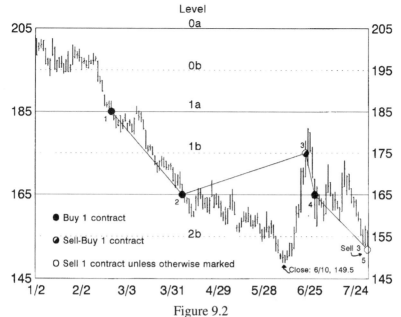

Figure 9.2
Interval Scale Trading[SM] with the Sell-Buy
August 1998 Soybean Meal
(Main Interval, 200 points; Intermediate Interval, 100 points
Starting Price, 185)

Table 9.3
Interval Scale Trading[SM] with the Sell-Buy
Summary of Buys and Sells for
August 1998 Soybean Meal
(See Figure 9.2)

Buy			Sell			Profit <Loss>
Figure Point	Date	Price	Figure Point	Date	Price	(Points)
1	2/20	185	5	7/31	151.9	<331>
2	4/06	165	3	6/23	175.0	100
3	6/23	175	5	7/31	151.9	<231>
4	6/29	165	5	7/31	151.9	<131>
					Total:	<593>

Table 9.4
Interval Scale Trading^{SM} with the Sell-Buy
Drawdown for August 1998 Soybean Meal
(See Figure 9.2)

Buy			Close on	Drawdown
Figure Point	Date	Price	6/10	(Points)
1	2/10	185	149.5	355
2	4/06	165	149.5	155
			Total:	510*

*The loss at the end of the contract life, 593 points, is greater than the drawdown during the contract life.

9.3. Interval Scale Trading^{SM} without the Sell-Buy

A. Trading Results

The buys and sells for **Interval Scale Trading^{SM}** without the sell-buy are shown in Figure 9.3 and summarized in Table 9.5.

Table 9.5
Interval Scale Trading^{SM} without the Sell-Buy
Summary of Buys and Sells for
August 1998 Soybean Meal
(See Figure 9.3)

Buy			Sell			Profit <Loss>
Figure Point	Date	Price	Figure Point	Date	Price	(Points)
1	2/20	185	4	7/31	151.9	<331>
2	4/06	165	4	7/31	151.9	<131>
3	6/29	165	4	7/31	151.9	<131>
					Total:	<593>

At $10.00 per point, the gross loss was:

Gross loss ($10.00 per point x 593 points) = <$5,930>

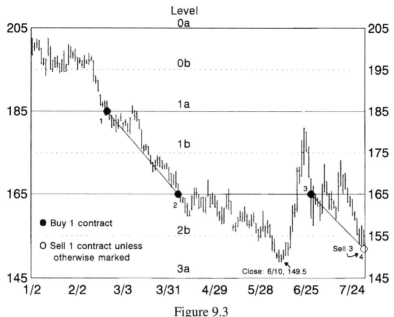

Figure 9.3
Interval Scale Trading[SM] without the Sell-Buy
August 1998 Soybean Meal
(Main Interval, 200 points; Intermediate Interval, 100 points
Starting Price, 185)

B. Drawdown and Capital Needs

The loss at the end of the contract was greater than the maximum drawdown during the contract life. We will calculate both of these values and then use the one that is the greatest to determine the percentage of capital reduction and rate of return.

1. Maximum Capital Needs During the Life of the Contract.

The maximum drawdown during the life of the contract for **Interval Scale Trading**[SM] of August 1998 Soybean Meal contract occurred at the close of 6/10/98. This drawdown is summarized in Table 9.6.

Table 9.6
Interval Scale Trading[SM] without the Sell-Buy
Drawdown for August
1998 Soybean Meal
(See Figure 9.3)

	Buy		Close on	Drawdown
Figure Point	Date	Price	6/10	(Points)
1	2/10	185	149.5	355
2	4/06	165	149.5	155
			Total:	510*

*The loss at the end of the contract life ,which was 593, is greater than the drawdown during the contract life.

The drawdown was 510 points. At $10.00 per point, this drawdown was:

Drawdown ($10.00 per point x 510 points) = $5,100

There were a total of two contracts in inventory at the close of 6/10/98. The initial margin for a contract of Soybean Meal is about $950. Therefore, the total capital needs at the close on 6/10 were:

Margin (2 contracts x $950 per contract)	$1,900
Drawdown:	$5,100

Total:	$7,000

2. Capital Needs at the Termination of the Contract

At contract end, the gross loss for this commodity contract was 593 points. At $10.00 per point, the loss was $5,930. A total of 3 contracts were held until the termination of trading. Therefore, the total capital needs just prior to contract termination were:

Margin (3 contract at $950 per contract):	$2,800
Drawdown:	$5,930

Total:	$8,730

Because the ending capital needs were larger than the capital needs during the contract life, we will use that figure ($8,730) for the remainder of the calculations.

The reduction in capital needs in comparison with classical scale trading for **Interval Scale Trading**^{SM} this contract is:

$$\frac{(\$12,000 - \$8,730)}{\$12,000} \times 100 = 27\%$$

Markets with no oscillations in their down phase show reductions in the 40-42% range (Chapters 6 and 7). A market with an oscillation in its down phase showed a 16% reduction (Chapter 8). This reduction value is intermediate, possibly reflecting the positioning of the oscillation in reference to this contract's price action.

C. Rate of Return for Interval Scale Trading^{SM} of August 1998 Soybean Meal

The gross loss from trading this contract was <$5,930>. A total of three round-turn commissions were needed. The maximum capital needs were $8,730. Therefore, the rate of return was:

$$\text{Rate of Return} = (<\$5,930>/\$8,730) \times 100 = <68\%>$$

The rate of return for **Interval Scale Trading**^{SM} was smaller than that of classical scale trading (<43%>) even though the drawdown was less. The lower rate of return for **Interval Scale Trading**^{SM} reflects the fact that a greater percentage of the capital needed to trade the contract was lost.

9.4. ParaScale Trading^{SM} Entry Followed by Interval Scale Trading^{SM}

A. Trading Results

The buys and sells for **ParaScale Trading**[SM] entry followed by **Interval Scale Trading**[SM] are given in Figure 9.4 and summarized in Table 9.7.

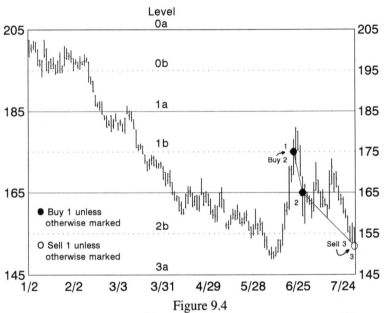

Figure 9.4
ParaScale Trading[SM] followed by **Interval Scale Trading**[SM]
August 1998 Soybean Meal
(Main Interval, 200 points; Intermediate Interval, 100 points
Starting Price, 185)

At $10.00 per point, the gross loss was:

Gross loss ($10.00 per point x 593 points) = <$5,930>

196

Table 9.7
ParaScale Trading[SM] followed by **Interval Scale Trading**[SM]
Summary of Buys and Sells for
August 1998 Soybean Meal
(See Figure 9.4)

Buy			Sell			Profit <Loss>
Figure Point	Date	Price	Figure Point	Date	Price	(Points)
1	6/23	175	3	7/31	151.9	<231>
1	6/23	175	3	7/31	151.9	<231>
2	6/29	165	3	7/31	151.9	<131>
					Total:	<593>

B. Drawdown and Capital Needs

The initial purchase was made after the contract had made its low on 6/10/98. Consequently, the maximum drawdown, 593 points, occurred at market end 7/31/98.

At contract end, the gross loss for this commodity contract was 593 points. At $10.00 per point, the loss was $5,930. A total of 3 contracts were held until the termination of trading. Therefore, the total capital needs just prior to contract termination were:

Margin (3 contract at $950 per contract):	$2,800
Drawdown:	$5,930

Total:	$8,730

The capital needs for the **ParaScale Trading**[SM] entry followed by **Interval Scale Trading**[SM] is the same as that of **Interval Scale Trading**[SM] alone.

The reduction in capital needs in comparison with classical scale trading for this contract is:

$$\frac{(\$12,000 - \$8,730)}{\$12,000} \times 100 = 27\%$$

This percentage reduction is the same as that of **Interval Scale Trading**[SM] alone.

C. Rate of Return for ParaScale Trading[SM] followed by Interval Scale Trading[SM] of August 1998 Soybean Meal

The gross loss from trading this contract was <$5,930> A total of three round-turn commissions were needed. The maximum capital needs were $8,780. Therefore, the rate of return was:

$$\text{Rate of Return} = (<\$5,930>/\$8,730) \times 100 = <68\%>$$

The rate of return for the **ParaScale Trading**[SM] entry followed by **Interval Scale Trading**[SM] is the same as that of **Interval Scale Trading**[SM] alone.

There was no advantage gained by using the **ParaScale Trading**[SM] entry method in this contract. The same amount of money was lost with and without the entry method and the drawdowns were identical. While there was no advantage in using the entry method, nothing was lost by using it.

9.5. ParaScale Trading[SM]

A. Trading Results

The buys and sells for **ParaScale Trading**[SM] are given in Figure 9.5 and summarized in Table 9.8.

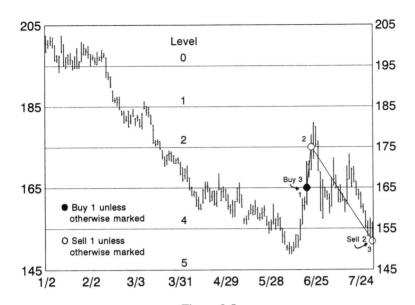

Figure 9.5
ParaScale Trading[SM]
August 1998 Soybean Meal
(Interval, 100 points; Starting Price, 185)

Table 9.8
ParaScale Trading[SM]
Summary of Buys and Sells for
August 1998 Soybean Meal
(See Figure 9.5)

Buy			Sell			Profit <Loss>
Figure Point	Date	Price	Figure Point	Date	Price	(Points)
1	6/19	165.0	3	7/31	151.9	<131>
1	6/19	165.0	3	7/31	151.9	<131>
1	6/19	165.0	2	6/23	175.0	100
					Total:	<162>

At $10.00 per point, the gross loss was:

Gross loss ($10.00 per point x <162> points) = <$1,620>

The **ParaScale Trading**[SM] signal for the initial purchase came before, and at a lower price, than the **ParaScale Trading**[SM] entry signal for **Interval Scale Trading**[SM]

(Section 9.4). Consequently, **ParaScale Trading**^{SM} had an oscillation profit (Point 1 to Point 2). Two contracts remained in inventory at contract termination.

B. Drawdown and Capital Needs

The maximum drawdown occurred at contract termination. Two contracts were in inventory and both were sold at 151.9. The drawdown is summarized in Table 9.9.

Table 9.9
ParaScale Trading^{SM}
Drawdown for August 1998 Soybean Meal
(See Figure 9.5)

Buy			Close on	Drawdown
Figure Point	Date	Price	7/31	(Points)
1	6/19	165.0	151.9	131
1	6/19	165.0	151.9	131
			Total:	262

At $10.00 per point, the drawdown was:

Drawdown ($10.00 per point x 262 points) = $2,620

Two contracts were in inventory at contract termination. The margin for a contract of Soybean Meal was about $950. Therefore, the total capital needs for **ParaScale Trading**^{SM} this contract were:

Margin (2 contracts at $950 per contract):	$1,900
Drawdown:	$2,620

Total:	$4,520

The reduction in capital needs in comparison with classical scale trading for this contract is:

$$\frac{(\$12,000 - \$4,520)}{\$12,000} \times 100 = 62\%$$

C. Rate of Return for ParaScale Trading^{SM} of August 1998 Soybean Meal

The gross loss from trading this contract was <$1620>. A total of three round-turn commissions were needed. The maximum capital needs were $4,520. Therefore, the rate of return was:

$$\text{Rate of Return} = (<\$1,620>/\$4,520) \times 100 = <35\%>$$

Within the scale trading family, **ParaScale Trading**^{SM} had the highest rate of return. It also had the smallest loss, the smallest capital needs, and the largest reduction of capital needs. This superior performance was due in part to the lower price of the initial purchase and in part that the market moved high enough after the initial purchase to allow a profit to be taken.

9.6. Summary of Scale Trading Results for August 1998 Soybean Meal

Table 9.10 provides a summary of the trading results for August 1998 Soybean Meal for the scale trading family discussed in this chapter. The **Interval Scale Trading**^{SM} results included in Table 9.10 refers to both **Interval Scale Trading**^{SM} with and without the sell-buy since their results are identical.

Table 9.10
Summary of Trading Results for
August 1998 Soybean Meal

	Classical Scale Trading	Interval Scale Trading^{SM}	ParaScale Trading^{SM} then Interval Scale Trading^{SM}	ParaScale Trading^{SM}
Gross Profit:	<$5,240>	<$5,930>	<$5,930>	<$1,620>
Number of Round Turn Commissions	6	3	3	3
Capital Needs:				
Margin:	$3,800	$2,800	$2,800	$1,900
Drawdown:	$8,200	$5,930	$5,930	$2,620
Total:	$12,000	$8,730	$8,730	$4,520
Reduction of Capital Needs:	--	27%	27%	62%
Rate of Return	<42%>	<68%>	<68%>	<35%>

Chapter 10

January 1998 Orange Juice.

A Rollover Example

January 1998 Orange Juice was chosen for the rollover example. This January contract moved down to a market low in October 1997. From there, the up phase began. All of the scale trading family showed a profit in this market. However, the up phase was insufficient to allow all of the contracts of all scale family members to be sold at a profit. Therefore, each has an example of one or more contracts that could be rolled over into a deferred month. May 1998 Orange Juice was chosen for the rollover month.

As in previous examples used in this book, in real time trading some of the trades taken toward the end of this contract would have been taken in a deferred contract. They were taken in this contract for consistency and for rollover examples. This procedure allows direct comparison of the results of the various scale trading family.

The one-third price for January 1998 Orange Juice was rounded to a starting price of 90.00. A little over seven months were traded, starting on 5/16/97 and ending on 12/31/97. The May 1998 contract was started on 12/1/97 and ended on 4/30/98. A 40-day moving average is shown on the May 1998 contract for those scale trading methods that employ it in their rollover procedure.

A contract of Orange Juice is 15,000 lbs with prices quoted in cents per pound. A minimum fluctuation is 0.05 ¢ per lb (5 points, $7.50). The data in this chapter is expressed in points (1 point = $1.50) where appropriate. The initial margin for a contract of Orange Juice is about $1,000.

10.1. Classical Scale Trading

A. Trading Results and Drawdown

The buys and sells for the classical scale trading of this commodity are shown in Figure 10.1 and summarized in Table 10.1.

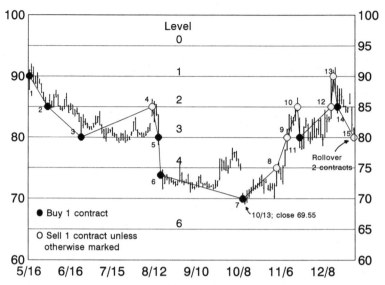

Figure 10.1
Classical Scale Trading
January 1998 Orange Juice
(Interval, 500 points; Starting price, 90.00)

Table 10.1
Classical Scale Trading
Summary of Buys and Sells for
January 1998 Orange Juice
(See Figure 10.1)

Buy			Sell			Profit <Loss>
Figure Point	Date	Price	Figure Point	Date	Price	(Points)
1	05/16	90.00	15	12/31	80.00	<1,000>
2	05/30	85.00	13	12/15	90.00	500
3	06/23	80.00	4	08/11	85.00	500
5	08/14	80.00	10	11/18	85.00	500
6	08/15	73.80	9	11/11	80.00	620
7	10/10	69.95	8	11/04	75.00	505
11	11/19	80.00	12	12/12	85.00	500
14	12/17	85.00	15	12/31	80.00	<500>
					Total:	1,625

At $1.50 per point, the gross profit was:

Gross profit ($1.50 per point x 1,625 points) = $2,437.

Two contracts were sold at the end of the contract for a total loss of 1,500 points. These are the two contracts that were rolled over into the May 1998 contract.

The drawdown for January 1998 Orange Juice is summarized in Table 10.2.

Table 10.2
Classical Scale Trading
Drawdown for
January 1998 Orange Juice
(See Figure 10.1)

	Buy		Close on	Drawdown
Figure Point	Date	Price	10/13	(Points)
1	05/16	90.00	69.55	2,045
2	05/30	85.00	69.55	1,545
5	08/14	80.00	69.55	1,045
6	08/15	73.80	69.55	425
7	10/10	69.95	69.55	40
Less Oscillation Profit				
3	06/23	80.00	85	<500*>
			Total:	4,600

*The profit of 500 points is enclosed in < > to show that it is subtracted from the drawdown.

At $1.50 per point, the drawdown on 10/13/97 was:

Drawdown ($1.50 per point x 4,600 points) = $6,900

A total of five contracts were in inventory at maximum drawdown. The margin for Orange Juice is about $1,000 per contract. Therefore, the capital needs at maximum drawdown was:

Margin (5 contracts x $1,000 per contract):	$5,000
Drawdown:	$6,900

Total:	$11,900

B. Rollover

Two contracts with a total loss of 1,500 points were rolled over into the May 1998 Orange Juice contract. For classical scale trading a rollover table is used to guide the trading. (See Section 2.12 and Table 2.4). The Rollover Table for January 1998 Orange Juice is shown in Table 10.3.

Table 10.3
Classical Scale Trading
Rollover Table for
January 1998 Orange Juice

Scale Entry Price	Close Out Price	Gain <Loss>	Original Profit Goal	Rollover Value	New Entry Price*	New Sell Price
90.00	80.00	<10.00>	5.00	15.00	85.10	100.10
85.00	80.00	<5.00>	5.00	10.00	85.10	95.10

*The May 1998 Orange Juice opening on 1/5/98.

Figure 10.2 shows the rollover month, May 1998 Orange Juice, with the rollover purchase and the two sells marked. The purchase was made on the open of 1/5/98, the next market day after the January contracts were sold (12/31/97).

The summary of the rollover buys and sells is given in Table 10.4.

Table 10.4
Summary of Rollover Buys and Sells
May 1998 Orange Juice

Buy			Sell			Profit <Loss>
Figure Point	Date	Price	Figure Point	Date	Price	(Points)
1	1/5	85.10	3	1/21	100.10	1,500
1	1/5	85.10	2	1/15	95.10	1,000
					Total:	2,500

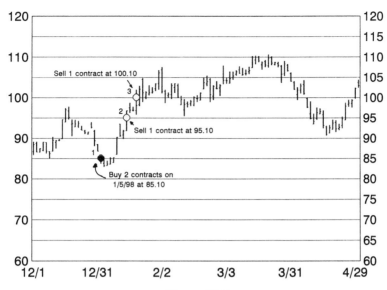

Figure 10.2
Classical Scale Trading Rollover Example
May 1998 Orange Juice

Combining the rollover profits with the profits from the original January trade, the combined profit was

Combined profit (in points) = 1,625 (January) + 2,500 (May) = 4,125 points

At $1.50 per point, the total profit from the original and rollover trades was

Total profit = ($1.50 per point x 4,125 points) = $6,187

The maximum capital needed on 10/13/97 was $11,900. A total of 10 round-turn commissions were required. The rate of return (excluding commissions) was:

Rate of return ($6,187/$11,900) = 52%

10.2. Interval Scale Trading^{SM} without the Sell-Buy

A. Trading Results and Drawdown

The buys and sells for **Interval Scale Trading^{SM}** without the sell-buy of January 1998 Orange Juice is shown in Figure 10.3 and summarized in Table 10.5

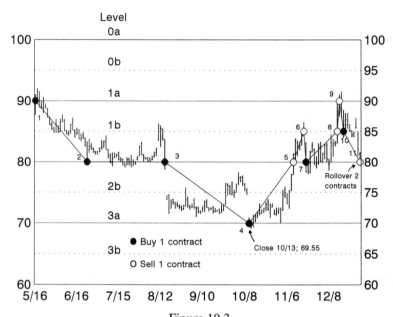

Figure 10.3
Interval Scale Trading^{SM} without the Sell-Buy
January 1998 Orange Juice
(Main Interval, 1,000 points; Intermediate Interval, 500 points;
Starting price, 90.00)

At $1.50 per point, the gross profit was:

Gross profit ($1.50 per point x 1,505 points) = $2,257

The difference in gross profit between classical scale and **Interval Scale Trading^{SM}** is 120 points ($180) and arises because of a fortuitous buy (a gap open below the buy point) in classical scale trading at Point 6 (Figure 10.1).

208

Table 10.5
Interval Scale Trading[SM] without the Sell-Buy
Summary of Buys and Sells for
January 1998 Orange Juice
(See Figure 10.3)

Buy			Sell			Profit <Loss>
Figure Point	Date	Price	Figure Point	Date	Price	(Points)
1	05/16	90.00	11	12/31	80.00	<1,000>
2	06/23	80.00	9	12/15	90.00	1,000
3	08/14	80.00	6	11/18	85.00	500
4	10/10	69.95	5	11/11	80.00	1,005
7	11/19	80.00	8	12/12	85.00	500
10	12/17	85.00	11	12/31	80.00	<500>
					Total:	1,505

As in the case of classical scale trading, two contracts were sold at the end of the contract for a total loss of 1,500 points. These are the two contracts that were rolled over into the May 1998 contract.

The drawdown for **Interval Scale Trading**[SM] of January 1998 Orange Juice is summarized in Table 10.6.

Table 10.6
Interval Scale Trading[SM] without the Sell-Buy
Drawdown for
January 1998 Orange Juice
(See Figure 10.3)

Buy			Close on	Drawdown
Figure Point	Date	Price	10/13	(Points)
1	05/16	90.00	69.55	2,045
2	06/23	80.00	69.55	1,045
3	08/14	80.00	69.55	1,045
4	10/10	69.95	69.55	40
			Total:	4,175

At $1.50 per point, the drawdown was:

209

$$\text{Drawdown (\$1.50 per point} \times \text{4,175 points)} = \$6,262$$

A total of four contracts were in inventory at maximum drawdown. The margin for a contract of Orange Juice is about $1,000. Therefore, the capital needs at maximum drawdown (excluding commissions) were:

Margin (4 contracts x $1,000 per contract):	$4,000
Drawdown:	$6,262

Total capital needs:	$10,262

In comparison with classical scale trading, the reduction in capital needs was:

$$\frac{(\$11,900 - 10,262)}{\$11,900} \times 100 = 13\%$$

This reduction is in line with the other reduction in capital needs (16%, July 1998 Pork Bellies) that was observed when there was an oscillation in the down phase of the market.

B. Rollover

Two contracts with a total loss of 1,500 points were rolled over into the May 1998 Orange Juice contract. For **Interval Scale Trading**^{SM} and **ParaScale Trading**^{SM}, we use an average-down method of calculating target prices for the rollover contracts. The calculations are shown below.

Rollover for Interval Scale Trading^{SM} of May 1998 Orange Juice
Number of contracts: 2
Total losses from the contracts: 1,500 points
Main Interval size: 1,000 points

Calculation of the Rollover Values

No profit from the rollover:

$$
\begin{aligned}
\text{Rollover value 1} &= \text{(Total loss)/ (Number of contracts)} \\
&= 1{,}500 \text{ points } /2 \\
&= 750 \text{ points (or 7.50 cents per lb)}
\end{aligned}
$$

One-half of a Main Interval profit per contract from the rollover:

$$
\begin{aligned}
\text{Rollover value 2} &= \text{(Rollover value 1)} + \text{(Main Interval }/2) \\
&= 750 \text{ points } + (1{,}000/2) \text{ points} \\
&= 750 \text{ points } + 500 \text{ points} \\
&= 1{,}250 \text{ points (or 12.50 cents per lb)}
\end{aligned}
$$

A full Main Interval profit per contract from the rollover:

$$
\begin{aligned}
\text{Rollover value 3} &= \text{Rollover value 1} + \text{Main Interval} \\
&= 750 \text{ points } + 1{,}000 \text{ points} \\
&= 1{,}750 \text{ points (or 17.50 cents per lb)}
\end{aligned}
$$

With **Interval Scale Trading**^{SM} and **ParaScale Trading**^{SM}, we do not enter the rollover position in the new contract until the market closes above the 40-day moving average. The first possible day the contracts could be rolled over was 1/5/98. However, the market was below the 40-day moving average at that time. Therefore, we remained out of the market.

The market closed above the 40 day moving average on 1/12/98. The next day's close was also above the moving average; therefore, we entered the market with the purchase of two contracts at 90.70 each. This provides our entry price and allows the calculation of the three target values.

$$
\begin{aligned}
\text{Target price 1} &= \text{Entry price} + \text{Rollover value 1 (in cents per lb)} \\
&= 90.70 + 7.5 \\
&= 98.2
\end{aligned}
$$

$$
\begin{aligned}
\text{Target price 2} &= \text{Entry price} + \text{Rollover value 2 (in cents per lb)} \\
&= 90.70 + 12.50 \\
&= 103.2
\end{aligned}
$$

$$
\begin{aligned}
\text{Target price 3} &= \text{Entry price} + \text{Rollover value 3 (in cents per lb)} \\
&= 90.70 + 17.50 \\
&= 108.2
\end{aligned}
$$

Figure 10.4 shows May 1998 Orange Juice with these prices marked on the chart along with the purchase price.

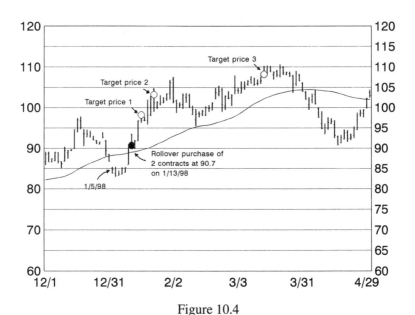

Figure 10.4
Rollover Example
Interval Scale Trading[SM]
May 1998 Orange Juice with 40-Day Moving Average

Unlike classical scale trading, there are three possibilities for rollover profit. Since each was possible, we will consider each individually.

Rollover with only recovery of losses.

Target price 1 was exceeded on 1/16/98 in the May contract. The two contracts would have been sold at a price of 98.20; therefore, the gross profit for one contract would have been:

Gross profit = 98.20 - 90.70 = 7.50 cents per lb or 750 points

With two contracts, the total gross profit would have been 1,500 points. Combined with the profit from the original January trade, the combined profit would have been:

Combined profit (points) = 1,505 (January) + 1,500 (May) = 3,005 points

At $1.50 per point, the gross profit would have been:

Gross profit ($1.50 per point x 3,005 points) = $4,507

The maximum capital needed was $10,262. Eight round-turn commissions were required for trading in the original and rollover months. The percentage return (excluding commissions) would have been:

Percentage return = ($4,507/$10,262) x 100 = 44%.

Rollover with recovery of losses plus one-half an interval of profit

Target price 2 was exceeded on 1/23/98 in the May contract. The two contracts would have been sold at a price of 103.20; therefore, the gross profit for one contract would have been:

Gross profit = 103.20 - 90.70 = 12.50 cents per lb or 1,250 points

With two contracts, the total gross profit would have been 2,500 points. Combined with the profit from the original January trade, the combined profit would have been:

Combined profit (points) = 1,505 (January) + 2,500 (May) = 4,005 points

At $1.50 per point, the gross profit would have been:

Gross profit ($1.50 per point x 4,005 points) = $6,007

The maximum capital needed was $10,262. Eight round-turn commissions were required for trading in the original and rollover months. The percentage return (excluding commissions) would have been:

Percentage return = ($6,007/$10,262) x 100 = 58%.

Rollover with recovery of losses plus one interval of profit.

Target price 3 was exceeded on 3/13/98 in the May contract. The two contracts would have been sold at a price of 108.20; therefore, the gross profit for one contract would have been:

Gross profit = 108.20 - 90.70 = 17.50 cents per lb or 1,750 points

With two contracts, the total gross profit would have been 3,500 points. Combined with the profit from the original January trade, the combined profit would have been:

Combined profit (points) = 1,505 (January) + 3,500 (May) = 5,005 points

At $1.50 per point, the gross profit would have been:

Gross profit ($1.50 per point x 5,005 points) = $7,507

The maximum capital needed was $10,262. Eight round-turn commissions were required for trading in the original and rollover months. The percentage return (excluding commissions) would have been:

Percentage return = ($7,507/$10,262) x 100 = 73%.

10.3. ParaScale Trading^{SM} Entry followed by Interval Scale Trading^{SM}

A. Trading Results and Drawdown

The buys and sells for **ParaScale Trading**^{SM} Entry followed by **Interval Scale Trading**^{SM} of January 1998 Orange Juice is shown in Figure 10.5. The profit, drawdown, capital needs, and rate of return are the same as those of **Interval Scale Trading**^{SM}. The pertinent data are summarized in Tables 10.7 and 10.8

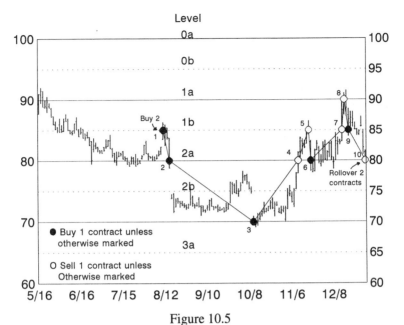

Figure 10.5
ParaScale Trading[SM] Entry followed by
Interval Scale Trading[SM] without the Sell-Buy
January 1998 Orange Juice
(Main Interval, 1,000 points; Intermediate Interval, 500 points;
Starting price, 90.00)

Table 10.7
ParaScale Trading[SM] Entry followed by
Interval Scale Trading[SM] without the Sell-Buy
Summary of Buys and Sells for
January 1998 Orange Juice
(See Figure 10.5)

Buy			Sell			Profit <Loss>
Figure Point	Date	Price	Figure Point	Date	Price	(Points)
1	08/11	85.00	10	12/31	80.00	<500>
1	08/11	85.00	8	12/15	90.00	500
2	08/14	80.00	5	11/18	85.00	500
3	10/10	69.95	4	11/11	80.00	1,005
6	11/19	80.00	7	12/12	85.00	500
9	12/17	85.00	10	12/31	80.00	<500>
					Total:	1,505

Table 10.8
ParaScale Trading^{SM} Entry followed by
Interval Scale Trading^{SM} without the Sell-Buy
Drawdown for
January 1998 Orange Juice
(See Figure 10.5)

| Figure Point | Buy | | Close on 10/13 | Drawdown (Points) |
	Date	Price		
1	08/11	85.00	69.55	1,545
1	08/11	85.00	69.55	1,545
2	08/14	80.00	69.55	1,045
3	10/10	69.95	69.55	40
			Total:	4,175

ParaScale Trading^{SM} Entry followed by
Interval Scale Trading^{SM} without the Sell-Buy

Gross profit: $2,257
Margin required at maximum drawdown: $4,000
Drawdown: $6,262
Total Capital needs: $10,262
Reduction in capital needs in comparison with classical
    scale trading: 13%

B. Rollover

There is one significant difference between **Interval Scale Trading**^{SM} with and without the **ParaScale Trading**^{SM} entry method and that is the losses that need to be rolled over. With **Interval Scale Trading**^{SM} by itself, the total losses were 1,500 points, while with **ParaScale Trading**^{SM} entry method, the losses were only 1,000 points. The difference is a result of the lower price of the first two purchases using the **ParaScale Trading**^{SM} entry. As a consequence, the rollover calculations and rate of returns will be different.

Rollover for ParaScale Trading[SM] followed by Interval Scale Trading[SM] of May 1998 Orange Juice

Number of contracts: 2
Total losses from the contracts: 1,000 points
Main Interval size: 1,000 points

Calculation of the Rollover Values

No profit from the rollover:

$$\text{Rollover value 1} = \text{(Total loss)/ (Number of contracts)}$$
$$= 1{,}000 \text{ points } /2$$
$$= 500 \text{ points (or 5.00 cents per lb)}$$

One-half of a Main Interval profit per contract from the rollover:
$$\text{Rollover value 2} = \text{(Rollover value 1)} + \text{(Main Interval } /2)$$
$$= 500 \text{ points } + (1{,}000/2) \text{ points}$$
$$= 500 \text{ points } + 500 \text{ points}$$
$$= 1{,}000 \text{ points (or 10.00 cents per lb)}$$

A full Main Interval profit per contract from the rollover:
$$\text{Rollover value 3} = \text{Rollover value 1} + \text{Main Interval}$$
$$= 500 \text{ points } + 1{,}000 \text{ points}$$
$$= 1{,}500 \text{ points (or 15.00 cents per lb)}$$

The market closed above the 40 day moving average on 1/12/98. The next day's close was also above the moving average; therefore, we entered the market with the purchase of two contracts at 90.70 each. This provides our entry price and allows the calculation of the three target values.

$$\text{Target price 1} = \text{Entry price} + \text{Rollover value 1 (in cents per lb)}$$
$$= 90.7 + 5.0$$
$$= 95.7$$

$$\text{Target price 2} = \text{Entry price} + \text{Rollover value 2 (in cents per lb)}$$
$$= 90.7 + 10.00$$
$$= 100.7$$

$$\text{Target price 3} = \text{Entry price} + \text{Rollover value 3 (in cents per lb)}$$
$$= 90.7 + 15.00$$
$$= 105.7$$

Figure 10.6 shows May 1998 Orange Juice with these prices marked on the chart along with the purchase price.

Unlike classical scale trading, there are three possibilities for rollover profit. Since each was possible, we will consider each individually.

Rollover with only recovery of losses.

Target price 1 was exceeded on 1/15/98 in the May contract. The two contracts would have been sold at a price of 95.70; therefore, the gross profit for one contract would have been:

Gross profit = 95.70 - 90.7 = 5.00 cents per lb or 500 points

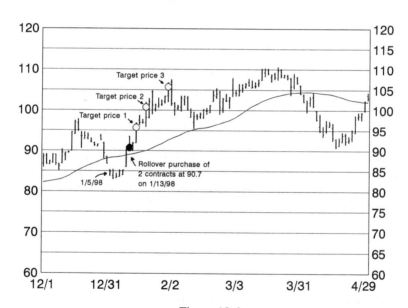

Figure 10.6
Rollover Example
ParaScale Trading^{SM} Entry followed by
Interval Scale Trading^{SM} without the Sell-Buy
May 1998 Orange Juice with 40-Day Moving Average

With two contracts, the total gross profit would have been 1,000 points. Combined with the profit from the original January trade, the combined profit would have been:

Combined profit (points) = 1,505 (January) + 1,000 (May) = 2,505 points

At $1.50 per point, the gross profit would have been:

Gross profit ($1.50 per point x 2,505 points) = $3,757

The maximum capital needed was $10,262. Eight round-turn commissions were required for trading in the original and rollover months. The percentage return (excluding commissions) would have been:

Percentage return = ($3,757/$10,262) x 100 = 37%.

Rollover with recovery of losses plus one-half an interval of profit

Target price 2 was exceeded on 1/21/98 in the May contract. The two contracts would have been sold at a price of 100.70; therefore, the gross profit for one contract would have been:

Gross profit = 100.70 - 90.70 = 10.00 cents per lb or 1,000 points

With two contracts, the total gross profit would have been 2,000 points. With the profit from the original January trade, the combined profit would have been:

Combined profit (points) = 1,505 (January) + 2,000 (May) = 3,505 points

At $1.50 per point, the gross profit would have been:

Gross profit ($1.50 per point x 3,505 points) = $5,257

The maximum capital needed was $10,262. Eight round-turn commissions were required for trading in the original and rollover months. The percentage return (excluding commissions) would have been:

Percentage return = ($5,257/$10,262) x 100 = 51%.

Rollover with recovery of losses plus one interval of profit.

Target price 3 was exceeded on 1/30/98 in the May contract. The two contracts would have been sold at a price of 105.7; therefore, the gross profit for one contract would have been:

Gross profit = 105.70 - 90.70 = 15.00 cents per lb or 1,500 points

With two contracts, the total gross profit would have been 3,000 points. Combined with the profit from the original January trade, the combined profit would have been:

Combined profit (points) = 1,505 (January) + 3,000 (May) = 4,505 points

At $1.50 per point, the gross profit would have been:

Gross profit ($1.50 per point x 4,505 points) = $6,757

The maximum capital needed was $10,262. Eight round-turn commissions were required for trading in the original and rollover months. The percentage return (excluding commissions) would have been:

Percentage return = ($6,757/$10,262) x 100 = 66%.

10.4. ParaScale Trading^{SM}

A. Trading Results and Drawdown

The buys and sells for **ParaScale Trading**^{SM} January 1998 Orange Juice are shown in Figure 10.7 and summarized in Table 10.9.

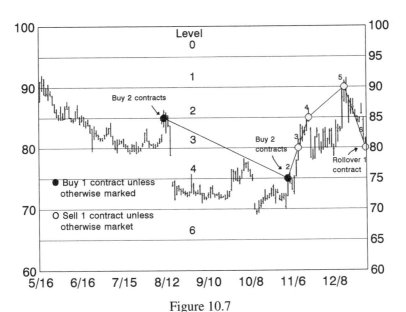

Figure 10.7
ParaScale Trading^{SM}
January 1998 Orange Juice
(Interval, 500 points; Starting price, 90.00)

Table 10.9
ParaScale Trading^{SM}
Summary of Buys and Sells for
January 1998 Orange Juice
(See Figure 10.7)

Buy			Sell			Profit <Loss>
Figure Point	Date	Price	Figure Point	Date	Price	(Points)
1	08/11	85.00	6	12/31	80.00	<500>
1	08/11	85.00	5	12/15	90.00	500
2	11/04	75.00	4	11/18	85.00	1,000
2	11/04	75.00	3	11/11	80.00	500
					Total:	1,500

At $1.50 per point, the gross profit was:

Gross profit ($1.50 per point x 1,500 points) = $2,250

Only one contract was sold at the end of the contract's life to a total loss of 500 points. This is the contract that was rolled over into the May 1998 contract.

The drawdown for **ParaScale Trading**^{SM} January 1998 Orange Juice is summarized in Table 10.10. Two of the four contracts purchased after the contract low did not contribute to the maximum drawdown. The two contracts that contributed to the maximum drawdown were purchased during an oscillation in the down phase of the market.

Table 10.10
ParaScale Trading^{SM}
Drawdown for
January 1998 Orange Juice
(See Figure 10.7)

Buy			Close on	Drawdown
Figure Point	Date	Price		(Points)
1	8/11	85.00	69.55	1,545
1	8/11	85.00	69.55	1,545
			Total:	3,090

At $1.50 per point, the drawdown on 10/13 was:

Drawdown ($1.50 per point x 3,090 points) = $4,635

A total of two contracts were in inventory at maximum drawdown. The margin for Orange Juice is about $1,000 per contract. Therefore, the capital needs at maximum drawdown was:

Margin (2 contracts x $1,000 per contract):	$2,000
Drawdown:	$4,635

Total:	$6,635

In comparison with classical scale trading, the reduction in capital needs was:

$$\frac{(\$11,900 - \$6,635)}{\$11,900} \times 100 = 44\%$$

This reduction is in line with the other reduction in capital needs (44%, July 1998 Pork Bellies) that was observed when there was an oscillation in the down phase of the market.

B. Rollover

One contract with a total loss of 500 points was rolled over into the May 1998 Orange Juice contract. For **Interval Scale Trading**[SM] and **ParaScale Trading**[SM] we use an average-down method of calculating the target prices for the rollover contracts. However, here, we only have one contract to rollover. Therefore, no averaging is possible. The calculations are shown below.

Rollover for ParaScale Trading[SM] of May 1998 Orange Juice
Number of contracts: 1
Total losses from the contracts: 1,500 points
Main Interval size: 500 points

Calculation of the Rollover Values

No profit from the rollover:

Rollover value 1 = (Total loss)/ (Number of contracts)
= 500 points /1
= 500 points (or 5.00 cents per lb)

One-half of a Main Interval profit per contract from the rollover:
Rollover value 2 = (Rollover value 1) + (Main Interval /2)
= 500 points + (500/2) points
= 500 points + 250 points
= 750 points (or 7.50 cents per lb)

A full Main Interval profit per contract from the rollover:
Rollover value 3 = Rollover value 1 + Main Interval
= 500 points + 500 points
= 1,000 points (or 10.00 cents per lb)

The market closed above the 40 day moving average on 1/12/98. The next day's close was also above the moving average; therefore, we entered the market with the purchase of two contracts at 90.70 each. This provides our entry price and allows the calculation of the three target values.

$$\begin{aligned} \text{Target price 1} &= \text{Entry price + Rollover value 1 (in cents per lb)} \\ &= 90.70 + 5.00 \\ &= 95.70 \end{aligned}$$

$$\begin{aligned} \text{Target price 2} &= \text{Entry price + Rollover value 2 (in cents per lb)} \\ &= 90.70 + 7.50 \\ &= 98.20 \end{aligned}$$

$$\begin{aligned} \text{Target price 3} &= \text{Entry price + Rollover value 3 (in cents per lb)} \\ &= 90.70 + 10.00 \\ &= 100.70 \end{aligned}$$

Figure 10.8 shows May 1998 Orange Juice with these prices marked on the chart along with the purchase price.

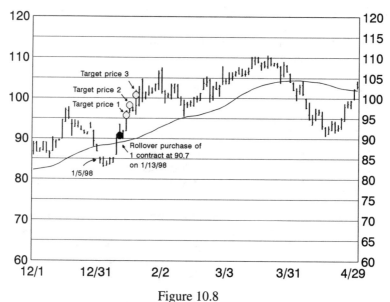

Figure 10.8
Rollover Example for **ParaScale Trading**[SM]
May 1998 Orange Juice with 40-Day Moving Average

Rollover with only recovery of losses.

Target price 1 was exceeded on 1/15/98 in the May contract. The contract would have been sold at a price of 95.70; therefore, the gross profit for the one contract would have been:

Gross profit = 95.70 - 90.70 = 5.00 cents per lb or 500 points

With the profit from the original January trade, the combined profit would have been:

Combined profit (points) = 1,500 (January) + 500 (May) = 2,000 points

At $1.50 per point, the gross profit would have been:

Gross profit ($1.50 per point x 2,000 points) = $3,000

The maximum capital needed was $6,635. Five round-turn commissions were required for trading in the original and rollover months. The percentage return (excluding commissions) would have been:

Percentage return = ($3,000/$6,635) x 100 = 45%.

Rollover with recovery of losses plus one-half an interval of profit

Target price 2 was exceeded on 1/16/98 in the May contract. The contract would have been sold at a price of 98.20; therefore, the gross profit for the one contract would have been:

Gross profit = 98.20 - 90.70 = 7.50 cents per lb or 750 points

With the profit from the original January trade, the combined profit would have been:

Combined profit (points) = 1,500 (January) + 750 (May) = 2,250 points

At $1.50 per point, the gross profit would have been:

Gross profit ($1.50 per point x 2,250 points) = $3,375

The maximum capital needed was $6,635. Five round-turn commissions were required for trading in the original and rollover months. The percentage return (excluding commissions) would have been:

Percentage return = ($3,375/$6,635) x 100 = 51%.

Rollover with recovery of losses plus one interval of profit.

Target price 3 was exceeded on 3/21/98 in the May contract. The contract would have been sold at a price of 100.70; therefore, the gross profit for the one contract would have been:

Gross profit = 100.7 - 90.70 = 10.00 cents per lb or 1,000 points

Combined with the profit from the original January trade, the combined profit would have been:

Combined profit (points) = 1,500 (January) + 1,000 (May) = 2,500 points

At $1.50 per point, the gross profit would have been:

Gross profit ($1.50 per point x 2,500 points) = $3,750

The maximum capital needed was $6,536. Five round-turn commissions were required for trading in the original and rollover months. The percentage return (excluding commissions) would have been:

Percentage return = ($3,750/$6,536) x 100 = 57%.

10.5. Summary of Scale Trading Results for January Orange Juice and its Rollover into May 1998 Orange Juice

Table 10.11 provides a summary of the trading results for January 1998 Orange Juice for the scale trading family discussed in this chapter.

Table 10.11
Summary of Trading Results for
January 1998 Orange Juice

	Classical Scale Trading	Interval Scale Trading^{SM}	ParaScale Trading^{SM} then Interval Scale Trading^{SM}	ParaScale Trading^{SM}
Gross Profit:	$2,437	$2,257	$2,257	$2,250
Number of Round Turn Commissions	8	6	6	4
Capital Needs:				
Margin:	$5,000	$4,000	$4,000	$2,000
Drawdown:	$6,900	$6,262	$6,262	$4,635
Total:	$11,900	$10,262	$10,262	$6,635
Reduction of Capital Needs:	--	13%	13%	44%
Rate of Return	20%	<22%>	<22%>	34%

All scale trading techniques were able to rollover into the May contract with profit. None required a second rollover. Table 10.12 summarizes the maximum profit available from the rollover and the total combined profit as well as the percentage return that would result from the combination of both the January and May contracts.

Table 10.12
Summary of Maximum Rollover Result
May 1998 Orange Juice

	Classical Scale Trading	**Interval Scale Trading**[SM]	**ParaScale Trading**[SM] then **Interval Scale Trading**[SM]	**ParaScale Trading**[SM]
Maximum Profit from the Rollover Contract	$3,750	$5,250	$4,500	$1,500
Total Combined Profit	$6,157	$7,507	$6,757	$3,750
Total Combined Percentage Return	52%	73%	66%	57%

D

F

G

I

ABOUT THE AUTHOR

Ralph J Fessenden, Ph. D., formerly the chairman of the University of Montana chemistry department, also has been a proprietary futures trader and systems developer since the 1950s. Dr. Fessenden retired from the University of Montana in May 1994 as professor emeritus after a 27 year career at the University. He now devotes his time to trading and the study of the markets. He is the author of a variety of books relating to trading in the futures markets.

BUSINESS REPLY MAIL

FIRST-CLASS MAIL   PERMIT NO.117   NAPLES FL

POSTAGE WILL BE PAID BY ADDRESSEE:

the
Beacon
companies

PO BOX 770883
NAPLES, FLORIDA 34107-9985

Yes, I'd like more information on:

Brokerage Services

- ☐ INTERVAL SCALE TRADING^{SM} method
- ☐ PARASCALE TRADING^{SM} method
- ☐ classical scale trading method
- ☐ options trading
- ☐ other types of trading

Managed Accounts

- ☐ individually managed accounts
- ☐ pool accounts
- ☐ IRA accounts

Other Services..........

- ☐ THE SCALE TRADER™ newsletter

Name _____

Address _____

City _____ State _____ Zip _____

Daytime Phone _____ Fax number _____

E-mail address _____

1-888-232-2668   941-594-5556   Fax 941-594-1006
beacon@scaletrader.com   www.scaletrader.com

*Please note that your information is for our records only and is completely confidential.